KRISHNA MOHAN AVANCHA

Stop Marketing, Start Helping Customer First marketting Secret Unveiled

The Secretts Unveiled: Series: Book 7

First edition

This book was professionally typeset on Reedsy.
Find out more at reedsy.com

Contents

1

Use marketing research to target a specific market

David Darmanin, Hotjar's CEO (and my chief), dispatched two new businesses before Hotjar took off—however, the two organizations bit the dust. Each time, he and his group went through months attempting to plan an astonishing new item and client experience, yet they fizzled on the grounds that they didn't have an away from what the market requested.

With Hotjar, they did things any other way. Long story short, they directed statistical surveying in the beginning phases to sort out what their shoppers truly needed, and they made (and keep on making) consistent upgrades dependent on their exploration.

In this blog entry, you'll figure out how to direct fast, compelling statistical surveying without recruiting an office—something many refers to as lean statistical surveying. It's simpler than you may suspect, and it very well may be done at any stage in an item's life-cycle.

To show you how it's done in reality, I've incorporated a statistical surveying model from Smallpdf. Smallpdf is a Swiss organization that pre-owned lean statistical surveying to lessen their instrument's mistake rate by 75% and help their Net Promoter Score® (NPS) by 1%.

What is the statistical surveying?

Statistical surveying (or advertising research) is an arrangement of methods used to accumulate data and better comprehend an organization's objective market. Organizations utilize this data to plan better items, improve client experience, and specialty a showcasing message that draws in quality leads and improves transformation rates.

Why is statistical surveying so important?

Without research, it's difficult to comprehend your clients. Without a doubt, you may have an overall thought of what their identity is and what they need, yet you need to burrow profound in the event that you need to win their dedication.

Here's the reason research matters...

Fixating on your clients is the best way to win. On the off chance that you couldn't care less about improving client experience, you'll lose expected clients to somebody who does.

The examination gives you the 'what,' however research gives the 'why.' Big information, client investigation, and dashboards can mention to you what individuals do at scale, yet no one but exploration can mention to you they're's opinion and why they do what they do. For instance, the examination can disclose to you that clients leave when they arrive at your evaluating page, however, no one but exploration can clarify why.

Exploration beats suspicions, patterns, thus called best practices. Have you ever viewed your partner's rally behind an awful choice? Ill-conceived notions are frequently the consequence of mystery, enthusiastic thinking, passing by best practices, and defaulting to the Highest Paid Person's Opinion (HiPPO). By tuning in to your clients and zeroing in on their customer experience, you're less inclined to get pulled off course.

Exploration shields you from arranging in a vacuum. Your group may be astounding, however, you and your partners essentially can't encounter your item the manner in which your clients do. Clients may utilize your item such that shocks you, and highlights that appear glaringly evident to you may confound them. Over arranging and declining to test your suppositions is an exercise in futility, cash, and exertion since you will probably have to make changes once your untested arrangement gets incorporated.

Favorable circumstances of lean statistical surveying

Lean User Experience (UX) plan is a model for constant improvement that depends on speedy, productive examination to comprehend client needs and test new highlights.

Lean statistical surveying can help you become more...

Productive: it gets you closer to your clients, quicker.

Practical: no compelling reason to recruit a costly showcasing firm to kick things off.

Serious: fast, amazing experiences can put your items on the bleeding edge.

4 regular statistical surveying techniques

There are loads of various ways you could direct statistical surveying and gather client information, yet you don't need to restrict yourself to only one exploration strategy. Four regular kinds of statistical surveying strategies incorporate reviews, interviews, center gatherings, and client perception.

1. Studies: the most regularly utilized

Studies ask clients a short arrangement of open-or-shut finished inquiries, which can be conveyed as an on-screen survey or through email. At the point when we asked 2,000 Customer Experience (CX) experts about their organization's way to deal with research, reviews end up being the most normally utilized statistical surveying procedure.

What makes online studies so well known?

They're simple and economical to direct, and you can do a ton of information assortment rapidly. Besides, the information is really direct to examine, in any event, when you need to break down open-finished inquiries whose answers may at first seem hard to sort.

2. Meetings: the smartest

Meetings are one-on-one discussions with individuals from your objective market. Nothing beats a vis-à-vis meet for jumping profound (and perusing non-verbal prompts), yet on the off chance that an in-person meeting is beyond the realm of imagination, video conferencing is a strong subsequent option.

Notwithstanding how you direct it, any sort of top to the bottom meeting will create huge advantages in understanding your objective market and clients.

What makes meets so clever?

By talking straightforwardly with an ideal client, you'll acquire more prominent compassion for their experience, and you can follow smart strings that can create a lot of 'Aha!' minutes.

3. Center gatherings: the most perilous

Center gatherings unite a painstakingly chosen gathering of individuals who fit an organization's objective market. A prepared arbitrator drives a discussion encompassing the item, client experience, as well as showcasing message to acquire further bits of knowledge.

What makes center gatherings so hazardous?

In case you're new to statistical surveying, I wouldn't suggest beginning with center gatherings. Doing it right is costly, and on the off chance that you cut corners, your examination could succumb to a wide range of blunders. Predominance inclination (when an intense member impacts the gathering) and mediator style predisposition (when distinctive arbitrator characters achieve various outcomes in a similar report) are two of the numerous ways your center gathering information could get slanted.

4. Perception: the most impressive

During a client perception meeting, somebody from the organization takes notes while they watch an ideal client draw in with their item (or a comparative item from a contender).

What mentions objective fact so astute and amazing?

'Fly-on-the-divider' perception is an incredible choice for center gatherings. It's more affordable, yet you'll see individuals connect with your item in a characteristic setting without affecting one another. The lone disadvantage is that you can't get inside their heads, so perception is no swap for client overviews and meetings.

The most effective method to direct statistical surveying (in a lean way)

The accompanying four stages will give you a strong comprehension of who your clients are and what they need from an organization like yours.

1. Make straightforward client personas

A client persona is a semi-anecdotal character dependent on psychographic and segment information from individuals who use sites and items like your own.

Instructions to get the information: use on-page or messaged reviews and meetings to comprehend your clients.

The most effective method to do it right: whatever study/inquiries addresses you ask, they should respond to the accompanying inquiries regarding the client:

Who right?

What is their primary objective?

What is their primary hindrance to accomplishing this objective?

Traps to maintain a strategic distance from:

Try not to pose such a large number of inquiries! Hold it to five or less (ideally three), else you'll immerse them, and they'll quit replying.

Try not to stress a lot over normal segment addresses like age or foundation. All things being equal, center around the job these individuals play (as it identifies with your item) and their objectives.

How Smallpdf did it: Smallpdf ran an on-page overview for possibly 14 days and got 1,000 answers, which uncovered that a significant number of their clients were clerical specialists, understudies, and educators. At that point they made straightforward client personas like this one for administrators:

Who right? Clerical specialists.

What is their primary objective? Making Word reports from a filtered, printed copy archive or a PDF where the source document was lost.

What is their primary boundary to accomplishing it? Changing over a filtered PDF doc to a Word document.

2. Lead observational exploration

Observational exploration includes taking notes while watching somebody utilize your item (or a comparable item).

Obvious versus secret perception

Obvious perception includes inquiring as to whether they'll allow you to watch them utilize your item. (Smallpdf did this with clerical specialists.)

Undercover perception implies considering clients 'in the wild' without them knowing. This possibly works on the off chance that you sell a sort of item that individuals use consistently, yet it offers the most perfect observational information since individuals regularly carry on diversely when they realize they're being viewed. (Smallpdf did this with college understudies.)

Tips to do it right:

Record a section in your field notes, alongside a timestamp, each time an occasion happens.

Make note of their work process, catching the 'what,' 'why,' and 'for whom' of each activity.

Traps to dodge:

Try not to record video or sound, paying little heed to your strategy (obvious or secret). In the event that they realize you're recording, it'll make them apprehensive. Furthermore, in the event that they don't have the foggiest idea? It's downright frightening.

Remember to disclose for what reason you'd prefer to notice them (for obvious perception). They're bound to collaborate in the event that you reveal to them you need to improve the item.

How Smallpdf did it: here's the way Smallpdf noticed two distinctive client personas.

Noticing understudies: Kristina Wagner, an Interaction Designer from Smallpdf, went to bistros and libraries at two nearby colleges and held up until she saw understudies doing PDF-related exercises. At that point, she watched and took notes in good ways.

One thing that struck her was simply the distinction between how understudies announced their exercises versus how they truly carried on (i.e., self-announcing predisposition). Understudies, she found, gone through hours talking, tuning in to music, or just gazing at a clear screen as opposed to working. At the point when she discovered understudies who were working, she recorded the errand they were performing and the product they were utilizing

Noticing clerical specialists: Kristina sent messages to administrators disclosing that she'd prefer to notice them at work, and she asked the individuals who consented to attempt to group their PDF work for her perception day.

Watching administrators work, she discovered that they habitually expected to filter records into PDF-organization and afterward convert those PDFs into Word docs. By noticing the difficulties administrators confronted, Smallpdf knew which items to focus on development.

3. Direct individual meetings

Meetings are one-on-one discussions with individuals from your objective market. They permit you to burrow profound and truly investigate their interests, which can prompt a wide range of disclosures.

Tips to do it right:

Act like a writer, not a salesman. As opposed to attempting to talk your organization up, get some information about their lives, their requirements, their dissatisfactions, and how an item like yours could help.

Listen more, talk less. Be interested.

Ask 'why?' so you can burrow further. Get into the points of interest and find out about their past conduct.

Record the discussion so you don't need to take notes and can zero in on the discussion. There are a lot of administrations that will interpret recorded discussions at a decent cost.

Traps to evade:

Try not to pose driving or stacked inquiries.

The main inquiry uncovers predisposition on your part and pushes them a specific way (e.g., "Have you exploited the stunning new highlights we just delivered?).

A stacked inquiry is one that sneaks in a presumption which, if false, would make it difficult to answer sincerely. For instance, we can't ask you, "What did you find generally helpful about this article?" without finding out if you found the article valuable in any case.

Be wary when getting some information about the future (or expectations of future conduct).

Studies recommend that individuals aren't truly adept at foreseeing their own future conduct. This is because of a few psychological inclinations, from the confused superiority bias(we're acceptable at think about what others will do, yet we by one way or another believe we're extraordinary), to the confidence predisposition (which makes us see things with rose-shaded glasses), to the 'hallucination of control' (which causes us to fail to remember the part of haphazardness in future occasions).

How Smallpdf did it: Kristina investigated her instructor client persona by talking with college educators at a neighborhood graduate school. She discovered that the school was generally paperless and once in a while utilized PDFs, so for a time, she proceeded onward to the administrators.

Somewhat of a setback? Sure. However, this story features a significant exercise! Now and again you follow a lead and miss the mark, so you need to make changes on the fly. Lean statistical surveying is tied in with getting strong, noteworthy experiences rapidly so you can change things and see what works.

4. Dissect the information (without suffocating in it)

The accompanying methods will help you fold your head over the information without losing yourself in it. Keep in mind, the purpose of lean statistical surveying is to discover speedy, significant experiences.

2

Make differentiation a priority

Separation permits you to offer better benefits than clients at a reasonable cost, making a mutually beneficial situation that can help the general productivity and feasibility of your business. Our exploration shows there are six essential approaches to separate, including item, administration, channels of appropriation, connections, notoriety/picture, and cost.

Notwithstanding, not all separation techniques are similarly powerful, and a few strategies might be more essential to put resources into than others to stand apart from the opposition. Peruse on to study these various procedures and the key preferences and detriments related to everyone.

Item Differentiation

Item separation is likely the most obvious. It incorporates real physical and saw contrasts, of which the last can be procured through publicizing. Item separation may appear as highlights, execution, adequacy (or the capacity of the item to do what it is suspected to do), meeting details, or various different standards. This is the overall territory that most B2B advertisers — and likely most purchaser advertisers too — invest most of their energy and dollars.

The issue, however, is that item separation is brief. It is strikingly simple to copy practically any item development. Obviously, the western world has a refined licensed innovation rights ethic and a general set of laws that gives copyright and patent assurance. From a pragmatic viewpoint, however, these don't present difficulties. Indeed, numerous organizations pick deliberately not to patent since it advises contenders precisely how to copy the favorable position. In the best case scenario, item development is secured for the life of the patent. To say the least, when a patent doesn't exist, anybody with enough money to purchase a machine might be a rival very quickly or weeks.

Administration Differentiation

Separation of administration incorporates conveyance and client assistance, yet any remaining supporting components of a business, for example, preparing, establishment, and simplicity of requesting. To many, these seem like the straightforward segments of a business — the hindering and handling or the fundamental components that don't need complexity. However, consider a systematic McDonald's. Like their Big Mac or not, they realize how to separate assistance. With not many special cases, you will get the very item and the very assistance at a McDonald's in Texas that you will get in Georgia, Connecticut, or California. What's more, in every area, the fries will be cooked the equivalent, have a similar measure of salt and be served up similarly as straight from the fryer.

Appropriation Differentiation

Channels of appropriation can likewise be a successful method for separation. Conveyance can give inclusion or accessibility, quick admittance to mastery, and more prominent simplicity of requesting, and more significant levels of the client or specialized assistance.

For some, producers confronting a divided market, it isn't achievable to arrive at the end client without the appropriation work. Building materials, for instance, need to some way or move from the processing plant to the contractual worker. Such items ordinarily travel through two phases of circulation including ace wholesalers, claim to fame sellers, and retailers.

Channels_of_Distribution_Figure_1.jpg

With adequate help — that is preparing, joint deals call, supporting writing, lead sharing, and so forth — a merchant can turn into an ardent partner constantly of the maker.

Indeed, even in a non-selective relationship, a submitted wholesaler can make an advantage through joint advancements, packaging, guarantee and administration backing, and specialized help. The time has come devouring and amazingly costly for a contender to pre-empt or copy this degree of separation.

Relationship Differentiation

A regularly disregarded method for separation is through organization faculty. Representatives, partners, or colleagues with client interfaces can give and exhibit capability, kindness, validity, dependability, and responsiveness. Answerable for executing everyday customer confronting correspondence, they are the linkage between the item and client. In the event that that linkage separates, the business is pulverized.

In numerous organizations, the salesperson, CSR, or the specialized help agent turns into a confided in the individual from the client's group, guaranteeing that the item is conveyed on schedule and functions as it should while settling any issues rapidly and precisely. Execution like this makes enthusiastic connections between the seller and the client.

This road of separation is firmly identified with administration, however centers explicitly around the individuals. Clients need to lead the business with individuals, not an organization. Building this relationship requires some serious energy, yet sets up an exceptionally separated position.

Picture/Reputation Differentiation

A few organizations set themselves apart by their picture either as a component of another separation road or as a different keyway. Regularly, the picture is made by different types of separation, for example, elevated levels of administration, unrivaled item quality, or execution.

The picture is controlled and overseen by images utilized in interchanges, promoting, and a wide range of media — composed, advanced, and sound, just as the environment of the actual spot where clients experience the business. This isn't restricted to retail organizations as it were.

A picture or notoriety can be an overwhelming obstacle for expected new participants. DuPont, for instance, by and large, has a solid picture as a specialized force to be reckoned with in practically all business sectors in which they partake. The organization utilizes countless designers, researchers, and item advancement specialists. Their salespeople regularly have a solid specialized instruction or foundation, and their items are situated as being driving edge. Milliken and Company have a comparative picture. For the possible new beginning up wishing to contend with such a juggernaut, regularly the solitary alternative is a kind of guerilla fighting.

The brand doesn't consequently separate an organization from its rivals. The brand needs to represent something, be perceived by the intended interest group, and convey something exceptional and unique in relation to the opposition. That takes a huge showcasing spending plan to pull off effectively. It is perceived that it takes seven reiterations of any message to try and be heard. Marking is considerably more than simply making a logo. It is the progressing correspondence of your offer is an important and successful manner.

With a little promoting spending plan, the sharpest, best methodology is to move away from a marking technique and towards a client-driven procedure. Pick a small bunch of clients that can drive the accomplishment of your business. That could be somewhere in the range of 3 to 4 or 15 to 20, yet it isn't hundreds. At that point center the entirety of your financial plan around these organizations. Give them precisely what they need, and show improvement over any other person can. You will expand a lot of their business, and they will become steadfast supporters and advertisers of your business.

Value Differentiation

Effectively contending on cost requires acknowledgment that each client has an alternate value they would pay for your item. Division and separation permit a business to verge on amplifying the expected income by offering each fragment a separated item at an alternate cost.

Value separation (or segregation) perceives that the estimation of products is an abstract reality, which shifts by the client, use event, and working climate. In the B2B world, most costs are dependent upon some sort of arrangement, and a few clients are set up to follow through on more than the predominant market cost. To put it plainly, value segregation permits a business to catch customer excess — the distinction between the sum purchasers are eager to pay for a decent or administration and the sum that they really pay.

Components to Consider for Differentiation

A distinction merits setting up when it meets, in any event, one of the accompanying measures:

- Important: the apparent advantage surpasses the expense
- Significant: conveys an advantage basic to progress
- Unmistakable: novel or offered in a particular way
- Unrivaled: better innovation, quicker

- Enthusiastic: binds to a center feeling — love, disdain, want
- Imparts: comprehended and obvious
- Preemptive: can't be effortlessly replicated
- Reasonable: clients can follow through on the greater expense
- Beneficial: commitment (edge times volume) surpasses the cost of distinction

Stay tuned for the following blog entry by Priority Metrics Groups, where we'll talk about winning differentiators dependent on exclusive study examination.

Get More Strategic Insights

Download MarketResearch.com's free white paper to find out about the estimation of statistical surveying and how master industry examination can help you stay in front of the opposition.

3

Take customer feedback at every step a priority

Need your business to stand apart from the opposition? Gain client criticism. It's the most dependable approach to improve the client experience. What's more, extraordinary client experience is critical to separating your business, expanding client devotion, and advancing brand support. A CEI survey even found that 86% of purchasers are eager to pay more for a superior client experience.

Acquiring client input, and eventually improving the client experience is likewise on each business' radar. Late exploration shows that 81% of organizations intend to zero in on acquiring client experiences this year. Nobody understands what your clients need more than your clients themselves.

So how would you acquire this significant client input? Follow these five key advances:

Stage 1: Know what you need to accomplish·

What precisely would you like to think about your clients' experience? Would you like to think about their cooperation with your staff, item quality, estimating, an assortment of items or administrations you offer, long periods of activity? The rundown can get pretty long, isn't that so? Pick close to 1-2 classes, for example, staff collaboration and item related inquiries, to jump into and adhere to those.

A huge load of inquiries in a single singular motion will overpower clients and their answers will come up short on the profundity you're searching for. Kill whatever's 'ideal to know' and just ask what you need to know to make enhancements.

Download our free retail client dependability achievement manual to figure out how to drive clients back 2x more.

Stage 2: Gather significant criticism

Criticism is useless in case you don't know how to manage it. For instance, knowing your consumer loyalty rating is a normal 8 out of 10 doesn't advise you precisely what your clients need you to improve. Creating your inquiries accurately is basic to getting the correct data that is valuable to your business.

To assemble and acquire noteworthy input, consistently incorporate subsequent inquiries like, "How could we deal with improve?," or "What did you like most about your experience?" You can get much more explicit by asking, "On a size of 1-5, was our staff inviting or inviting?," or "How might you want to get with us in regards to unique advancements or occasions?"

Stage 3: Gather however much input as could reasonably be expected, and make the cycle simple

There are endless approaches to gather client input. Make the cycle as simple as could be expected under the circumstances, and pick any/the entirety of the accompanying choices that will give your input endeavors the most openness.

Online studies (sent by means of email, site, blog, the interface on receipt) – Use online devices like SurveyMonkey, GetFeedback, or even Google Forms and email overviews to your present client base. Incorporate review joins on your site or blog (spring up modules can assist with this too). What's more, remember a connection to your study for receipts if conceivable.

Online media – Use Facebook's survey device: Facebook Questions, tweet inquiries to the majority on Twitter, connect by means of LinkedIn Groups, make outwardly engaging pictures pushing your review and pin them on Pinterest or post them on Instagram – Be certain to incorporate a connection.

Audit destinations (Yelp, Google, Angie's List, and so forth) – Gather data from surveys individuals have just composed on different audit locales. Answer to different reactions, positive and negative to assemble more information. They'll be astounded and glad to realize you care about their experience.

In-person meets or via telephone – Ask inquiries at the register, or as a client is leaving the business. On the off chance that you have individuals bringing in to make arrangements or request food/items, inquire as to whether you can attach two or three inquiries when wrapping up the call. Send an email or instant message also asking clients for face to face or via telephone interviews in return for a rebate.

In-store input/remark cards – We energetically suggest utilizing criticism designs like online overviews, as printed remark cards have a few set-backs, nonetheless, on the off chance that you actually decide to take this course: place these on tables, counters, close to the register, front passageway, or pass them out with the check. Permit clients to stay unknown by setting the remark card in a container, instead of giving it straightforwardly to a worker.

Keep in mind, criticism will assist your business with improving, and request-ing it shows the clients you give it a second thought. Mean to accumulate criticism from in any event 20% of your present client base, or 20% of your target group. Get however many reactions as would be prudent from new and steadfast clients the same.

Stage 4: Give impetus

Criticism endeavors are upgraded by motivations. On the off chance that you plan on requiring over 5 minutes of your clients' time, give your clients a prize; the better the prize, the better. Set your spending plan and attempt one of these thoughts:

10 fortunate clients get a $5-$10 coupon

For each reaction, we'll give $1 to a good cause

X haphazardly chose victors to get a $50 gift voucher

The initial 20 respondents get a half rebate on their next request

Stage 5: Define the following stages

When every one of your reactions has come in, it's the ideal opportunity for the main advance: make changes depending on your input. You'll fabricate trust and cultivate unwaveringness by responding to your client's criticism with genuine enhancements. Take the most mainstream demands from your reactions and apply them to your business. Offer the exploration with your representatives and let your clients realize you heard them and are making their experience your need.

By executing these five key strides to acquiring criticism, and making a move, your client experience, item, or business will be nothing not exactly first-rate. We as of late made enhancements to our own items and devices dependent on client input, and the reaction has been glowingly sure – Feedback is quite amazing! Have you made changes to your own business, client support, or item dependent on client input?

4

Ask the right questions

There is a familiar aphorism that says one should look to comprehend prior to trying to be perceived. I state, we have two ears and just one mouth for an explanation - in light of the fact that we need to listen twice as much at this very moment.

Correspondence is the main aptitude a human can create - and this is doubly valid for pioneers. Yet, listening isn't aimless. You are likely to keen on tuning in for explicit data. This implies that to convey well, you need to pose the perfect inquiry and ask it at the perfect time. Some unacceptable inquiry is nearly ensured to create some unacceptable answer. The correct inquiry posed at some unacceptable time - in some unacceptable setting, while there are squeezing interruptions, requested from some unacceptable individual - is similarly pointless.

Here are the means I utilize when I am prepared to tune in and need explicit data.

1. Try not to pose logical inquiries.

A non-serious inquiry is hyperbole as an inquiry. They are normally asked to make a point as opposed to evoke an answer. Such inquiries are not actually questions yet are intended to drive somebody into a particular reaction. This wastes your time.

2. Ask neighborly, explaining questions.

A decent inquiry allows you to more readily comprehend the circumstance, and this requires not putting individuals on edge. Belittling an individual once in a while delivers fair input.

3. Try not to set snares.

Try not to call the audience out. There is an old joke where a constituent inquired as to whether he had stopped beating his significant other. The inquiry was intended to drive a forswearing of some kind not to give significant data. Articulate your inquiries without raising a crate around them.

4. Pose open-finished inquiries.

Scarcely any inquiries can be accurately replied with yes/no, A/B, forward/in reverse. Twofold answers are regularly invalid. It is smarter to pose an open-finished inquiry - one without counterfeit limits - and to offer the respondent opportunity to respond with the proper degree of detail and subtlety. Open-finished inquiries additionally permit the audience more prominent solace with the correspondence, since they are not compelled to settle on fragmented decisions.

5. Be thankful.

Thank the individual for their reaction. All things considered, you will probably need their bits of knowledge once more.

6. Dodge pressure.

Answers gave during tense circumstances are frequently helpless ones. In the event that the circumstance is tense however not a crisis, at that point holding up a brief timeframe improves the chances of a quality answer, since the respondent will have time and center to mull over.

7. Try not to be excessively immediate.

Regardless of whether you are attempting to find a particular solution, being too immediate and too explicit can prompt inflexible answers. Rather than, "Would it be a good idea for us to make item An or B?" ask, "What item is the market requesting, and how do our choices satisfy that need?"

8. Sitting quietly is sometimes best.

Be a willing audience. In any event, when the other individual isn't talking, correspondence is as yet dynamic. Chill out between inquiries to give you and the other individual chance to decompress. This makes your correspondences less like a cross-examination, regardless of whether it is a reality discovering mission.

The majority of all, pose inquiries as you might want to be asked them. Require that concise second to consider how you would address the inquiry you are going to pose, and in the event that you feel awkward, at that point you need to reword it.

5

Put customers first instead of product

Most organizations have a type of witticism that echoes the "client first" notion: Customer is King, The Customer is Always Right, and so forth Albeit void proverbs may flourish, there is an absence of useful data on what it precisely intends to put the client first.

Organizations that dominate at making consumer loyalty flourish while others endure, however, what does this resemble all things considered? Instead of dubious explanations, organizations need to actualize strategies and systems to put the client at the focal point of the organization. Here are 6 different ways your organization can put your client first.

1Create a client persona

By knowing your demographic and making a client profile, or persona, you can make approaches and practices that will better market and oblige them. By having an away from who you are working for, you can save important time, cash, and energy in your organization.

Start by having an overall thought of who is utilizing your item or administration. Pose yourself a few inquiries about your objective clients. Is it true that you are working with partnerships or people? Cutting-edge new businesses, or bigger, more settled organizations? While it is conceivable to have a wide scope of clients, for example, working with the two companies and people, by isolating them into classes you can outline how you intend to market and administration each sort of client.

Next, make things a stride further by considering what precisely your optimal client would need. For example, would they lean toward individualized help, or smoothed out approaches? Would your client incline toward speed and effectiveness, or top to bottom assistance? It very well may be a loss for your organization to have every minute of every day client support telephone line when your client would lean toward having an inside and out FAQ on your site for their inquiries, or the other way around.

By knowing who you like to and really work with you can quit going around aimlessly and sitting around attempting to assuage everybody. You can focus on what your ordinary client needs and foresee their necessities.

2Empower your client support to twist the standards

Permitting the forefront of client care to settle on judgment decisions will establish a climate where everybody is attempting to help the client, as opposed to causing them to feel powerless in being compassionate and obliging to the client. By permitting client support to twist the standards, your worker will feel engaged to sidestep a strategy on the off chance that it is by organization esteems (reasonableness, for instance).

It additionally will shield them from feeling oppressed to exacting approach and sending each client protest to the board. By taking care of unique circumstances as opposed to sending them along, the cutting edge of client care will save the executives time and energy.

In any case, enabling client support doesn't mean essentially permitting client care to part with the merchandise. Having a set approach that permits client assistance to do so will regularly bring about a deficiency of income. Engaging client care implies permitting them to settle on judgment decisions dependent on individual circumstances.

Preparing client assistance with "assuming at that point" arranging permits them to settle on judgment decisions without burning through one or the other administration or the client's time. Otherwise called usage expectation, "assuming at that point" arranging gives client support general rules that can be utilized in different circumstances, (for example, if the client has been standing by longer than 10 minutes to see a sales rep, at that point offer a drink). It permits client assistance to envision a client's necessities and increment the consumer loyalty.

3Start all hands uphold

The requirements of the client ought not to stop at deals or client assistance. Regardless of whether a piece of IT, the executives, or Human Resources, having a feeling of the client's interests, needs, and needs will make a more engaged and client-driven organization.

Amazon is an incredible illustration of establishing a climate that revolves around the client. It is a prerequisite that everybody takes a turn working in client assistance regardless of their area of expertise. President Jeff Bezos accepts that it makes better sympathy for the client, so consistently even the upper administration will set aside the effort to be prepared in client support.

By having the whole organization work in client support eventually, everybody gets an opportunity to tune in to the client and get away from what they need. It would then be able to shape each part of the organization from how the executives make strategies to how IT composes code. The most ideal approach to permit workers to put clients initially is by permitting everybody an opportunity to tune in to the client.

4Spread images of client center

Images can be incredible suggestions to workers of the organization's qualities. It can move the center and fortify a client-driven climate.

Once more, Amazon gives an incredible model. During its initial days, Bezos would place an unfilled seat in each gathering to speak to the client. It served to strengthen to everybody in that gathering precisely who they were working for and expected to intrigue. Right now, they have representatives prepared to speak to the client's suppositions and concerns. Heads should test out their plans to that individual and prevail upon them most importantly.

pyramid of forefront workers, center administration, and top administration

They rearranged the executive's pyramid.

The Inverted Pyramid can likewise fill in as a ground-breaking image that fortifies organization esteems. It was broadly re-established by The Home Depot CEO Frank Blake while turning the organization around after the 2007 downturn.

In the Inverted Pyramid, the CEO and upper administration are put at the base, where they uphold bleeding-edge representatives who all eventually uphold the client. Having a visual image, for example, the pyramid where workers can routinely see it, (for example, the lunchroom) underscores the organization's esteems, (for example, the idea of worker administration) in an exceptionally commonsense way. It additionally fills in as a steady update the representatives uphold each other to serve the client.

5Promote straightforwardness

It is the grievous truth of business that it isn't generally conceivable to oblige each client demand. Clients can get angry and absurd. In some cases, such a large number of clients have an excessive number of solicitations. In these cases, adhering to a "client is in every case right" approach can detrimentally affect the organization.

At the point when you can't give the client what they need, it is imperative to give them an unmistakable motivation behind why and handle the circumstance with straightforwardness. Clients need to feel heard and considered regardless of whether their solicitations are not conceded. Telling the client why the current approach is set up permits them to get the master plan.

Most clients will be all the more agreement if they are explained. Harvard directed an investigation where three kinds of individuals requested to cut in line for a copier: one that basically requested to cut, one that requested to cut since he was in a surge, and one that essentially disclosed he expected to slice to make duplicates. In the primary form, 60% of individuals let him cut. In the second, 94% of individuals permitted the scientist to cut and 93% of individuals let the specialist in the third form cut, even though he gave a non-reason.

chart about the connection between explanations behind cutting in line and achievement rate

As the investigation illustrates, the explanation itself isn't as significant as just having one. Regardless of whether it may not sound good to the client, they will frequently like the straightforwardness.

Similarly, contemplates have demonstrated that clients are bound to be tolerant if they can see improvement being made for their benefit. Called the work deception, clients won't be disturbed pausing on the off chance that they feel that they are not being disregarded and can see that work is being accomplished for them. Straightforwardness can conquer numerous client support leaps and will comfort the client.

6Ask the 5 Whys

Created by Taiichi Ōno and utilized by Toyota, the 5 Why procedure permits client assistance to get to the foundation of any difficulty that may emerge and help keep it from happening once more. As opposed to hastily managing a difficult circumstance, the 5 Why Technique necessitates that they keep on inquiring as to why a circumstance emerged to more readily reveal insight into the arrangements and cycles that could be an issue. It is so-named because it regularly takes 5 "why's" to get to the primary driver of an issue.

The result of utilizing the method relies upon the information and tirelessness of the individuals in question. The object isn't to lay fault with any one individual, yet rather to check whether some sure strategies or methods are not functioning admirably or maybe don't exist. By getting to the center of the issue, it permits organizations to put resources into surveying and tweaking their cycles just when required.

Putting the client first methods more than surrendering to each client's interest. It takes a definite examination of the very organizational structure. It is imperative to initially know who your client is: comprehend their inquiries, needs, and worries to best market and oblige them.

Each individual from the organization should be included and smart, and even the bleeding edge of client care should be prepared to foresee the client's requirements. Be clear and forthright with clients so they can comprehend what is happening and why. Likewise, take a gander at cycles and approaches through the 5 Why Technique.

It is such a "Client First" organization that genuinely leaves clients fulfilled and organizations flourishing as opposed to rambling void proverbs that make different organizations wallow.

6

Engage with your customers in personal ways

For quite a long time, one-off advertising efforts were the greatest game around.

Since the ascent of the Internet, nonetheless—and, specifically, the ascent of online media—client conduct has changed drastically. Not just have web-based media become a fundamental apparatus for any advertising procedure (practically 50% of Facebook clients have "suggested" a brand), clients today likewise anticipate that their relationship with brands should go past the utilization estimation of their items.

Add Insight to your inbox.

We'll send you one email seven days with content you really need to peruse, curated by the Insight group.

For Mohan Sawhney, clinical educator of promoting and McCormick Foundation Chair of Technology at the Kellogg School, that implies it is the ideal opportunity for showcasing pioneers to grasp an alternate methodology.

Rather than the conventional "push" model of advertising efforts, commitment showcasing pulls individuals in by recounting stories, driving discussions, and tending to client needs and interests. The objective is to include clients in a more profound, more supported relationship with a given item or brand. "On the off chance that you just converse with clients about what you sell them, they have the alternative of blocking out," Sawhney says. "The witticism for commitment advertising is, 'Ask not how you can sell, but rather how you can help.'"

Here are five key tips for organizations looking to genuinely draw in their clients:

1. Offer clients genuine worth.

"Commitment promoting implies driving with content, not items," Sawhney says. What's more, that substance should be truly valuable to your clients for it to be an important commitment procedure.

"It's publicizing as an administration, instead of promoting as interference," Sawhney says. "Basically, you're offering clients esteem in return for their consideration."

Marketo, a supplier of showcasing computerization arrangements, offers an extensive arrangement of "Complete Guides" to help advertisers ace themes like advanced promoting, email advertising, social promoting, and advertising measurements. Rather than selling its foundation, Marketo looks to exhort and illuminate its clients and accordingly acquire the option to discuss its items. connection, an application made by Valspar Paint, offers virtual one-on-one paint discussions with an expert shading advisor who makes a redid shading plan customized to every member's space.

2. Fabricate a local area.

"A critical piece of commitment advertising is giving clients a chance for an exchange—with your image, however with one another," Sawhney says. You can kick the discussion off by requesting assessments and experiences, saying something regarding fascinating patterns, and uniting clients in online social-sharing networks.

"It's promoting as an administration, rather than publicizing as interference. Basically, you're offering clients esteem in return for their consideration."

Nike customarily depended on media publicizing to advance its idea of "drawing out the competitor in you." Recently it moved towards customized client assistance. As opposed to placing the entirety of its assets into a solitary promotion crusade for tennis shoes, Nike presently publicizes by offering clients exercise guidance and causing them to assemble online networks around the topic of wellness. Nike +, a site intended to make it simple to follow one's wellness progress, is essential for this new exertion.

American Express has adopted a comparable strategy to local area building. The organization made "OPEN Forum" in 2007, an online local area to help entrepreneurs develop their business by offering experiences, assets, and systems administration openings. By getting sorted out this stage for a developing local area of business people, the organization put itself at the front line of web-based media showcasing—a large number of organizations partake, and many follow the discussion on Twitter—and gave its image a critical lift. OPEN Forum is currently the top wellspring of leads for new business card individuals for American Express.

"At the point when clients draw in with you via online media, you can use their dedication to your image," Sawhney says. "Large numbers of them will be the evangelists that will help spread the word."

3. Rouse individuals.

"Individuals esteem valuable data and accommodation," Aditya says, "yet they additionally need to be propelled!"

One approach to rouse clients is to share your image's vision. Corning, a glass organization, put out a video called "A Day Made of Glass," which exhibits the motivating prospects of a day soon when the cutting edge glass it produces is in the homes and workplaces of ordinary clients. "You're attempting to portray the future that is rousing and show that you assume a significant part in that future," Sawhney says. This is particularly important for organizations that are attempting to work cutting-edge innovation.

Another approach to motivate is to make your image a specialist of social effect. In 2013, Chipotle delivered "The Scarecrow," an energized film that was profoundly condemning of manufacturing plant cultivating and started banter over food honesty. Starbucks has delivered comparable recordings advancing reasonable exchange espresso. Furthermore, barely any promoting activities have been more fruitful than that of Toms, the online business organization that guarantees on the off chance that you purchase a couple of its shoes, it will give a couple to a helpless kid someplace on the planet.

4. Give amusement esteem.

Notwithstanding being roused, clients like to be engaged—a tremendous open door for commitment advertising.

Take the case of "Where's My Wallet," an intuitive web-based game Commonwealth Bank utilized as an approach to advance its new Cardless Cash Technology in Australia. The game, which was available to anybody, highlighted an all-encompassing guide of Sydney; the goal was to discover one of 100 "lost wallets" covered up in the city, each containing a $200 reward. Victors needed to go to a Commonwealth ATM to guarantee their prize utilizing the Cardless Cash item. During the initial ten days of ongoing interaction, "Where's My Wallet" got 43,000 exceptional guests who went through on normal 12 minutes on the site.

Marriot International has likewise taken advantage of the energy for web-based media gaming by dispatching "My Marriot Hotel," a Facebook game that welcomes players to deal with their own virtual inn. For Marriot, this is both a promoting apparatus and HR procedure: notwithstanding creating interest in the Marriot brand, the game is intended to make in staff positions more appealing, particularly in nations where such positions are viewed as humble.

5. Make all the difference for the discussion.

Part of having a "consistently on" way to deal with promoting is that you are in steady discourse with clients.

To do this well requires regular development. It likewise implies remaining pertinent and receptive to client issues as they emerge. Profoundly responsive organizations rush to stop administration issues from the beginning through careful interchanges—taking off advertising goofs that can rapidly turn into a web sensation from all around associated clients.

In the event that showcasing works best when clients feel like they have a veritable connection with a brand—one that is intriguing, commonly advantageous, and consistent—that relationship should be maintained.

"A definitive objective of commitment is to construct a passionate association with the brand," Aditya says. "It's a cycle that prompts closeness and backing. It is anything but a solitary exchange, yet a continuous discussion. You can't anticipate that clients should tune in just when you have an item to dispatch. You need to have a consistent presence."

7

Find the right balance between personalization and Privacy

I n the course of the most recent decade or thereabouts, buyers have built up a convoluted relationship with innovation and protection. From one perspective, information and innovation have made it simpler to give customized online encounters. Nonetheless, individuals are getting increasingly more worried about protection.

Entrepreneurs and advertisers regularly end up strolling a fine line to give purchasers the personalization and protection they need. An as of late delivered study can help entrepreneurs and advertisers discover a balance between security and personalization.

A study from Virent shows the idea of the contention. As per the investigation's discoveries, of the in excess of 24,000 buyers studied, 80% said they like administrations that are customized to their necessities. Be that as it may, such a personalization expects organizations to utilize client information, yet shoppers are careful about the manner in which their private data is put away.

As per the Virent overview, 89 percent of buyers additionally need to realize how organizations keep their own data security and 86 percent demand that they should know when their information is given to outsiders.

"Organizations have a troublesome difficult exercise to haggle between security, straightforwardness, and customized insight. It's something that associations across all areas need to get right or danger losing significant clients," said Ryan Hollenbeck Verint SVP worldwide showcasing and client experience program chief support. "The present brands should attempt to guarantee more prominent straightforwardness over the utilization of client information and assemble trust and trust in this inexorably testing climate."

The need to ensure client information and console shoppers about the manner in which their information is dealt with is something that numerous entrepreneurs and advertisers knew about before the investigation even started. More than 11,000 organizations were spoken to among the overview respondents, and of these, 94 percent said it is significant that their clients be consoled their information is secure and 96 percent comprehend they need to caution clients if their information is to be given to outsiders.

At the point when four out of five or nine out of 10 shoppers feel a specific path about something, entrepreneurs have a minimal decision yet give a valiant effort to meet buyer assumptions. On account of information and security, it implies taking endeavors to utilize innovation appropriately and considering how buyers will feel about the manners in which their information is being utilized.

It's imperative to remember that since innovation makes something conceivable doesn't mean it's something a business ought to do. There are a lot of instances of organizations utilizing information in new manners that, while in fact stunning, dismiss clients by being too nosy. Facebook appears to end up in such a circumstance like clockwork or thereabouts.

Also, in different cases, entrepreneurs and purchasers the same are ignorant of the potential security issues until they are abused by others. To represent,

Amazon is as of now confronting a circumstance where the information from their continually listening Echo item is being looked for a criminal examination. To innovation can be a twofold edged blade for retailers and advertisers, something the analysts at Virent likewise remarked on.

"It boils down to getting the rudiments right, utilizing innovation and investigation to all the more likely comprehend what's truly on the brains of clients, and afterward attempting to help guarantee the correct assets are set up to address developing necessities and prerequisites," said Marije Gould, Verint VP, EMEA showcasing, as per media reports.

Entrepreneur and advertisers end up at a fascinating junction with regards to history. There has at no other time been when data about buyers was so natural to acquire thus close to home that organizations should have been this worried about protection issues. However, since we are in such a period, retailers need to act appropriately so their organizations can make due to what's to come.

8

Curate the best experiences by listening rather than talking

In the present cutting edge, rapid, high-stress world, correspondence is more significant than ever, yet we appear to dedicate less and less an ideal opportunity to truly tuning in to each other. Certified listening has become an uncommon blessing—the endowment of time. It helps fabricate connections, take care of issues, guarantee to understand, resolve clashes, and improve exactness. At work, powerful listening implies fewer mistakes and less sat around idly. At home, it creates clever, independent children who can tackle their own issues. Listening assembles companionships and vocations. It sets aside cash and relationships.

Here are 10 hints to assist you in creating viable listening abilities.

Stage 1: Face the speaker and keep in touch.

Conversing with somebody while they check the room, study a PC screen, or look out the window resembles attempting to hit a moving objective. What amount of the individual's separated consideration you are really getting? 50%? Five percent? If the individual was your kid, you may interest, "Take a gander at me when I'm conversing with you," however that is not such a thing we state to a sweetheart, companion, or associate.

In most Western societies, eye to eye connection is viewed as a fundamental element of successful correspondence. At the point when we talk, we look at one another without flinching. That doesn't imply that you can't carry on a discussion from across the room, or from another room, yet on the off chance that the discussion proceeds for any period of time, you (or the other individual) will get up and move. The craving for better correspondence arranges you.

Do your conversational accomplices the kindness of going to confront them. Set aside papers, books, the telephone, and different interruptions. Take a gander at them, regardless of whether they don't take a gander at you. Timidity, vulnerability, disgrace, blame, or different feelings, alongside social restrictions, can restrain eye to eye connection in certain individuals under certain conditions. The reason the other person, however, stays centered yourself.

Stage 2: Be mindful, yet loose.

Since you've visually connected, unwind. You don't need to gaze steadily at the other individual. You can turn away occasionally and continue as an ordinary individual. The significant thing is to be mindful. The word reference says that to "join in" someone else intends to:

- be available
- give consideration
- apply or direct yourself
- focus
- stay prepared to serve

Intellectually screen out interruptions, similar to foundation action and clamor. Likewise, do whatever it takes not to zero in on the speaker's inflection or discourse quirks to where they become interruptions. At last, don't be diverted by your own contemplations, sentiments, or predispositions.

Stage 3: Keep a receptive outlook.

Tune in without deciding on the other individual or intellectually censuring the things she advises you. On the off chance that what she says cautions you, feel free to feel frightened, however, don't state to yourself, "All things considered, that was a dumb move." As soon as you enjoy critical bemusements, you've undermined your adequacy as an audience.

Tune in without making a hasty judgment. Recall that the speaker is utilizing language to speak to the contemplations and emotions inside her mind. You don't have the foggiest idea what those contemplations and sentiments are and the lone way you'll discover is by tuning in.

Try not to be a sentence-grabber. At times my accomplice can't slow his psychological speed enough to listen adequately, so he attempts to accelerate mine by hindering and completing my sentences. This generally lends him way misguided, because he is following his own line of reasoning and doesn't realize where my musings are going. After a few rounds of this, I typically ask, "Would you like to have this discussion without help from anyone else, or would you like to hear what I need to state?" I wouldn't do that with everybody, except it works with him.

Stage 4: Listen to the words and attempt to picture what the speaker is stating.

Permit your psyche to make a psychological model of the data being imparted. Regardless of whether a strict picture or a course of action of unique ideas, your cerebrum will accomplish the vital work if you stay centered, with faculties completely ready. When tuning in for significant length, focus on, and recollect watchwords and expressions.

At the point when it's your chance to tune in, don't invest the energy arranging what to state straightaway. You can't practice and tune in simultaneously. Contemplate what the other individual is stating.

At last, focus on the thing that is being stated, regardless of whether it exhausts you. On the off chance that your contemplations begin to meander, quickly drive yourself to pull together.

Stage 5: Don't hinder and don't force your "answers."

Youngsters used to be instructed that it's discourteous to interfere. I don't know that message is getting across any longer. Unquestionably the inverse is being displayed on most of the television shows and reality programs where noisy, forceful, in-your-face conduct is excused, if not energized.

Hindering sends an assortment of messages. It says:

"I'm a higher priority than you are."

"What I need to state is all the more intriguing, exact, or important."

"I don't actually mind your opinion."

"I don't possess energy for your assessment."

"This isn't a discussion, it's a challenge, and I will win."

We as a whole might suspect and talk at various rates. If you are a fast scholar and a spry talker, the weight is on you to loosen up your speed for the more slow, more smart communicator—or for the person who experiences difficulty communicating.

When tuning in to somebody talk about an issue, abstain from recommending arrangements. A large portion of us doesn't need your recommendation at any rate. If we do, we'll request it. The greater part of us wants to sort out our own answers. We need you to tune in and assist us with doing that. Someplace route down the line, if you are totally overflowing with a splendid arrangement, at any rate, get the speaker's authorization. Ask, "Might you want to hear my thoughts?"

Stage 6: Wait for the speaker to delay to pose explaining inquiries.

At the point when you don't get something, obviously, you ought to request that the speaker disclose it to you. But instead, then interfere, stand by until the speaker stops. At that point say something like, "Back up a second. I didn't comprehend the thing you just said about... "

Stage 7: Ask addresses just to guarantee to understand.

At lunch, a partner is energetically educating you concerning her excursion to Vermont and all the superb things she did and saw. Throughout this narrative, she refers that she invested some energy with a shared companion. You bounce in with, "Gracious, I haven't got with Alice in a very long time. How is she?" and, much the same as that, conversation movements to Alice and her separation, and the helpless children, which prompts a correlation of care laws, and before you know it an hour is gone and Vermont is ancient history.

This specific conversational attack happens constantly. Our inquiries lead individuals in bearings that have nothing to do with where they thought they were going. In some cases we work our way back to the first theme, however frequently we don't.

At the point when you notice that your inquiry has driven the speaker adrift, assume liability for getting the discussion in the groove again by saying something like, "It was extraordinary to catch wind of Alice, however, reveal to me more about your experience in Vermont."

Stage 8: Try to feel what the speaker is feeling.

On the off chance that you feel dismal when the individual with whom you are talking communicates pity, happy when she communicates delight, unfortunate when she depicts her apprehensions—and pass on those emotions through your outward appearances and words—at that point, your adequacy as an audience is guaranteed. Sympathy is the essence of good tuning in.

To encounter sympathy, you need to place yourself in the other individual's place and permit yourself to feel what it resembles to be her at that point. This is certainly not something simple to do. It takes energy and fixation. Yet, it is a liberal and supportive activity, and it encourages correspondence like nothing else does.

Stage 9: Give the speaker ordinary input.

Show that you comprehend where the speaker is coming from by mirroring the speaker's emotions. "You should be excited!" "What an awful experience for you." "I can see that you are confounded." If the speaker's emotions are covered up or hazy, at that point every so often reword the substance of the message. Or then again gesture and show your comprehension through proper outward appearances and a periodic all around planned "gee" or "uh-huh."

The thought is to give the speaker some evidence that you are tuning in, and that you are following her line of reasoning—not off enjoying your own dreams while she converses with the ether.

In assignment circumstances, whether or not at work or home, consistently repeat directions and messages to be certain you see effectively.

Stage 10: Pay regard for what isn't said—to nonverbal signals.

On the off chance that you prohibit email, most of the direct correspondence is likely nonverbal. We gather a lot of data about one another without saying a word. Significantly via phone, you can adapt nearly as much about an individual from the tone and rhythm of her voice than from anything she says. At the point when I converse with my closest companion, it doesn't make a difference what we talk about, if I hear a lilt and giggling in her voice, I feel consoled that she's progressing nicely.

Vis-à-vis with an individual, you can recognize excitement, fatigue, or disturbance rapidly in the articulation around the eyes, the arrangement of the mouth, the slant of the shoulders. These are hints you can't disregard. When tuning in, recall that words pass on just a small amount of the message.

Listening Skills Exercise: Summarize, Summarize, Summarize!

For at any rate multi-week, toward the finish of each discussion where data is traded, close with an outline explanation. In discussions that bring about arrangements about future commitments or exercises, summing up won't just guarantee a precise finish, it will feel totally regular. In discussions that do exclude arrangements, if summing up feels abnormal simply clarify that you are doing it as an activity.

9

Make flexibility and convenience a priority

B2B vendors and supply affixes will in general invest a ton of energy estimating inside cycles and not investing enough energy into holding outside ones under control. Outreach groups receive an item or administration focused methodology, which means their key choices center around what they have to bring to the table with the point of expanding deals. At the point when they do follow their clients' purchasing propensities, it typically starts and finishes with the buy recurrence, item type, and request history. This kind of information, while important, doesn't disclose to us much about client feeling and the soundness of our client connections – that is, the place where we could improve.

What is a Customer-Focused Strategy?

While apparently evident and simple to execute on a superficial level, understanding where you remain in the client's eyes expects you to have all around characterized measures that start at the production network the executives level and end with the conveyance driver. If these cycles are very much sharpened, your clients will return, buy a greater amount of your item, and enlighten others concerning your image. Moreover, the information doesn't lie, as client-centered stockpile chains are dominating their partners on all fronts:

store network change

How to Create a Customer-Focused Brand?

A client-centered brand puts the client experience as the main piece of working together. It includes enhancing each client touchpoint, be it pre-deal, retail location, and after the deal to guarantee consumer loyalty consistently. We'll take a gander at six systems supply chains and B2B organizations can use to improve their client-centered methodology.

1. Make a client-centered culture

client-driven definition

Building a client culture is a concentrated exertion that begins from the highest point of the association – most explicitly with the board. A solid client center stems from arrangements and innovations that make it simple for representatives to shape associations with clients. Everybody in the group should have a firm comprehension of how their jobs influence the client experience, and how their practices enable client dedication and commitment.

Select administration

For an organization to be client-centered, it should initially have client-centered administration. This is normally designated to a CCO (boss client official) who is responsible for client-driven methodologies and cycles inside the association. Client officials go about as client advocates, imparting improvements around client concerns, and search for approaches to streamline the client venture map.

Account for thoughts

Go past tuning in to client concerns and gathering input. Show your representatives to be proactive and distinguish what clients acknowledge, esteem, and react decidedly to. Set up meetings to generate new ideas to skip thoughts around. Your procedure can incorporate things like personalization alternatives, advancements, or another way to deal with client support, things a quality CRM framework can assist you with.

Separate storehouses

Knowing your promoting technique deals direction, and what your clients need will empower you to situate yourself to all the more likely offer some incentive. By dividing information among eCommerce, CRM, ERP, WHM, acquirement, bookkeeping, and different frameworks, you'll get a definitive perceivability into activities. Alternately, being uninformed about these essential cycles will just damage your capacity to advance client-centricity inside your association.

Put resources into innovation

Developing client assumptions are filled with innovation. Portable is an enormous piece of our lives, information educated dynamic is all over the place, and AI vows to take work off the shoulders of advertisers, salesmen, and inventory network experts. With the patterns in distant work, self-booking innovation, and the ability to offer representatives more noteworthy self-rule can likewise encourage client needs, and offer sympathetic, proactive assistance.

Illustration of a client-centered advertising procedure

Numerous client-driven associations urge workers to go the additional mile to cause clients to feel incredible. Zappos broadly engages workers to do whatever they feel is the correct intention to guarantee client joy. If your financial plan doesn't permit that, occasionally, even the littlest motion works. "There's an inn that goes the additional mile to cause visitors to feel extra good," shares Martin Schulz from Airfocus. "They place a decent morning, great evening, and great night tangle at their entryway. This says a lot to clients who are there to loosen up and move away from their bustling lives. While a little signal, it's something they don't get somewhere else, so they have more motivations to continue to return to the lodging."

2. Accumulate and offer client information broad

client-centered difficulties

Each association is unique and the way and sort of information it gathers on clients will differ. Regardless of whether it's very own information, commitment designs, conditional subtleties, or client input, the information will assist you with being client-driven. That is the place where your devices, for example, your CRM, eCommerce stage, promoting robotization devices, and even AI chatbots would all be able to assume a job in empowering more point by point, individual discussions.

Gather deals information

Your business information holds the way to novel shopping encounters for each client. Information, for example, the agitate rate, the net advertiser score, and the client lifetime esteem are some broad measurements that measure client centricity. By consolidating deals and criticism information from your CRM and eCommerce frameworks – and sharing them across divisions – everybody sees how the client sees your image.

Client division

Client division gives organizations a superior comprehension of their market and clients. Besides understanding what sort of clients buy what item, division gives marks a thought of client commitment at a granular level. This can reveal undiscovered business openings, and help brands settle on essential choices without influencing other client fragments accidentally.

Client venture

Each phase of the client venture should be checked regularly and changed by keeping up the client-centered methodology. By keeping a nearby watch on client ventures, you can reveal patterns, plunges in commitment, or rubbing focuses, and work rapidly to correct them. Over the long run, this can construct faithfulness and long haul consumer loyalty, which will bring about more references.

A client center procedure requires the correct instruments

Putting information at the focal point of their client-centered system has paid off for B2B correspondence expert GetVoIP. After executing a CRM to help accumulate and examine applicable client information, tying it up to an email promoting device and Google Analytics, they got a remarkable perspective on client action. This information permitted them to assemble an email rundown of more than 100,000 supporters, help site traffic, and increment income.

3. Put resources into the client experience of online channels

client experience-b2b-purchaser

To make progress in your client-driven activities, it's critical to comprehend the inspirations and wants of your clients. As the portion of online B2B deals expands, client assumptions around the client experience develop and moves with it. Despite what industry you're in or who your clients are if the client experience is deficient with regards to, they'll mull over working with you not far off.

Personalization

A customized suggestion or markdown may pull in a B2C customer, however, B2B purchasers search for additional. Associations are keen on eCommerce self-administration entrances that are customized to them. Organizations need their own item inventories, evaluating, and checkout inclinations. In addition to the fact that it saves time, yet it builds accommodation and encourages them to buy or repurchase the correct things rapidly.

oro-imaginative

Straightforwardness

Straightforwardness isn't just about guaranteeing clients that crude materials come from feasible sources. It's tied in with imparting essential information at the ideal time. At the point when you demonstrate unavailable things on item pages or rundown rough restocking or delivery times, clients have less motivation to get disappointed. An ERP coordination can help you update stock information to your eCommerce site.

Client assistance

Client assistance, much the same as personalization, is anything but a one-size-fits-all methodology. It requires the correct client assistance devices and giving representatives self-rule to offer the most ideal help. For instance, OroCommerce permits eCommerce staff to sign in for the client to more readily see any issue at the client profile level.

Client support as a feature of a client-centered procedure

"Several years back we won an agreement with an organization that wound up bringing us more than $100,000," says Simone of Growing Together exponentially Ltd. "It was no simple accomplishment, as it took us three months to get the agreement. This time was spent understanding the more profound real factors of the business and talking to every individual from the outreach group just as the chiefs. We did this for nothing and without assurances of winning the agreement. Eventually, we had the option to make a modified suggestion that put us on top of other more dependable competitors."

4. Organize client maintenance

client maintenance client approach

Notably, keeping clients is simpler than securing existing ones. Hence, maintenance is a major piece of any client-driven procedure. Your agitate rate, rehash buy rate, existing client development rate, and the adequacy of relationship-building techniques will disclose to you how well you are getting along. Developing these measurements requires keeping a nearby watch of your client's drawn-out necessities, and acting rapidly to help them as their necessities change.

Use a CRM

One reason why numerous organizations battle to get client-centricity right is the staggering measure of client information now accessible. Numerous associations just don't have the correct devices and advances to assist them with achieving this. An adjustable CRM framework is one such apparatus that permits brands to section, profile, and target clients with the correct messages.

Train for progress

To be client-driven, outreach groups should change how they consider deals. Measurements, for example, pipeline and income streams are significant, yet so is helping, being sympathetic, and understanding client trouble spots. Numerous client-driven organizations to practice the entire organization uphold. They get deals, however promoting, item, and designing groups get a break from their errands, and find out about regular client protests.

Showcasing arrangement

At the point when the vast majority talk about adjusting deals and showcasing, they are proposing bringing together the lead the board cycle across offices. This implies being on the same wavelength of following and overseeing income openings, regardless of whether forthcoming or current – from age to its transformation into a client relationship. Coordinating CRM and eCommerce instruments together improves lead perceivability, which expands the viability of showcasing, deals, and client achievement endeavors.

The client center worked around client trust and correspondence

It's an extraordinary inclination when clients trust your capacity to convey quality regardless. "Primary to our methodology is building trust and responsibility with our customers from the very beginning and it has taken care of different occasions," says Maggie Bolt of The Poirier Group. "In one commitment, we zeroed in on guaranteeing the customers' necessities were met even to the detriment of our own benefit. This customer saw this exertion, which brought about them reconnecting with us commonly, referring to us to different customers." This methodology has given them rehash clients during financial declines – clients that might have handily gone to contenders.

5. Sell dependent on worth, not items or cost

client development esteem

Rather than amplifying the item or bringing down the value, center around how you convey an incentive to clients. Since sales reps are at the forefront of client communications, they should change that incentive as indicated by the client and circumstance. On the off chance that clients are intrigued, they'll need to understand what the item does, how it can help them, and what the aftereffects of that help will be, in genuine terms.

Tune in to clients

Compelling client listening is a top upper hand. That is the reason conveying and tuning in to client input oftentimes and consistently ought to be each client-driven brand's need. Regardless of whether that is leading overviews, apportioning time for one-on-one meetings, or keeping an SMS line or online media account open to gather input, it's imperative to consistently be on top of client concerns.

Make openings

With enough client information and examination added to your repertoire, you can produce a nitty-gritty image of what clients are searching for. When that is set up, you can put the client's advantage in everything your outreach group does. This accomplishes something beyond making encounters that clients are probably going to appreciate, as you can likewise find strategies that create unsurprising results and rehash their utilization.

Sell encounters

Organizations that place clients at the cutting edge comprehend the force of a pre-deal question. By posing the correct inquiries, for example, "How might I assist you with being beneficial today?" client confronting groups can make the deal, yet study the client's circumstance, and rapidly interface the appropriate response with something important that they can offer.

Settle a trouble spot

On the off chance that you need to consummate client correspondence, you can train your business staff to join sympathy with tending to client problem areas. This takes subtlety and specialty since it requires first distinguishing challenges clients manage each day while giving an answer that carries an incentive to them actually.

Worth driven client center systems, all things considered

One listening hardware retailer adopted an exceptional strategy to its client's problem areas. "It is hard for chapels, historical centers, and instruction foundations to pick assistive listening gear as the highlights are language loaded," says Will Ward of AssistiveListeningHQ. "Numerous establishments are completely confounded concerning what hardware they truly need. To begin with, I tended to this problem area by making inside and out aides explicit to every one of these establishments. At that point, I added a complementary number with the expectation of complimentary interviews. When I help them out, they are glad to purchase from my organization, alluding different clients to me simultaneously!"

6. Smooth out the inventory network

client-driven store network

Numerous clients request lower costs, quicker conveyance, and more prominent straightforwardness. Surrendering clients to date data on their conveyance remains a solid differentiator, for example, when their things leave the stockroom, administration focus, and when it shows up at the client's objective. This pattern is accelerating the digitalization of supply chains and presents advances, for example, ongoing following, progressed examination, and more noteworthy start to finish perceivability of all parts of satisfaction.

Request arranging

Appropriate interest and stock arranging rely upon the cautious investigation of your business history, value-based information, just as data from your stock, providers, distribution centers, and outside market patterns. As any of these components change, your interest in arranging figures should be refreshed also.

Request the executives

Perceivability into client orders helps eCommerce organizations decide how to satisfy them given the client. For instance, requests can be satisfied with each pick, piece picking, case picking, or bed picking. The favorable circumstances and burdens of every strategy ought to be powerfully examined and upgraded for present status conditions.

Distribution center administration

After a request is settled, the pressing and transportation cycles can initiate. Bungling these means can adversely affect the client experience. Your frameworks should keep an impeccably created SKU numbering framework, a precise picking measure that gets the thing delivered to its last objective as fast as could be expected under the circumstances.

Different satisfaction channels

The "omnichannel" pattern is taking the client experience as well as the production network industry by storm. Numerous huge retailers have just grasped omnichannel supply chains by offering the choice to purchase on the web and get face to face in a particular area. Working in different equal satisfaction channels makes it simpler to offer the speed and comfort clients may anticipate.

Client center models in personalization

A few associations take client centricity to the following level by incorporating it into their item. "We need to give a completely redid experience to every client," says Damien from AI-based personality confirmation organization Shufti Pro. "From the preliminary arrangement to arrangement incorporation and valuing plan, everything is adjustable. We saw our leads increment as we commanded the notice of numerous organizations that required planned arrangements. It additionally turned into our serious edge, as the adaptability to customize the entire item, from highlights to cycle to valuing made us genuinely novel available."

For what reason does a client-centered methodology matter?

Clients these days are only occasionally set up to buy amounts providers might want to supply, at a time determined by the provider, in the structure favored by the provider. This is fantastically clarified in Tony Hines' book Supply Chain Strategies, where he focuses on the significance of client center and the "seven clients Vs" that organizations should offer to clients: esteem, volume instability, speed, assortment, changeability, perceivability, virtuosity.

There's no single system that shows the client center. To be fruitful, B2B dealers should zero in on their way of life, information, client experience, maintenance, esteem, and their production network structures. That is, associations should consider their own client centricity as well as the client-driven nature of others that make up the inventory network organization. It's really at that time brands can utilize the aggregate center, techniques, and activities that advantage the end client.

<h1 style="text-align:center">10</h1>

Use buyer personas to better understand customers needs and necessities

Characterizing a purchaser persona (additionally called a client persona, crowd persona, or advertising persona) causes you to make substance to more readily focus on your optimal client.

As a social advertiser—or any advertiser, besides—it's anything but difficult to become mixed up in the subtleties of following your most recent commitment rates and missions. Purchaser personas remind you to put your crowd's needs constantly in front of your own.

What is a purchaser persona?

A purchaser persona is a nitty-gritty depiction of somebody who speaks to your intended interest group. This is definitely not a genuine client, however an anecdotal individual who epitomizes the qualities of your best-expected clients.

You'll give this client persona a name, segment subtleties, interests, and conduct qualities. You'll comprehend their objectives, problem areas, and purchasing behaviors.

You can give them a face utilizing stock photography. A few organizations have ventured to such an extreme as to make cardboard patterns of their purchaser personas to make them a genuine presence inside the workplace.

The thought is to consider and address this model client as though they were a genuine individual. This permits you to create showcasing messages focused on explicitly them. Your purchaser persona will manage everything from item advancement to your image voice to the social channels you use.

Since various gatherings of individuals may purchase your items for various reasons, you may have to make more than one purchaser persona. You can't become more acquainted with each client or prospect exclusively. However, you can make a client persona to speak to each section of your client base.

How your business should utilize purchaser or crowd personas

1. Reexamine your work from the client's point of view

Advertisers time after time utilize corporate-talk and a lot of trendy expressions that don't actually mean anything. Purchaser personas can assist you with dodging that trap by reminding you to consider the genuine people who read your social posts and draw in with your substance.

Purchaser personas keep you zeroed in on tending to client needs rather than your own.

Consider your purchaser personas each time you settle on a choice about your social showcasing technique (or by and large advertising methodology).

Does another mission address the requirements and objectives of at any rate one of your purchaser personas? If not, you have a valid justification to reexamine your arrangement, regardless of how energizing it very well might be.

Construct your social methodology dependent on aiding your personas meet their objectives, and you'll fabricate a bond with the genuine clients they speak to. It's tied in with boosting deals while making brand reliability and trust.

2. Focus on your social promotions all the more viably

Social promoting offers unimaginably nitty-gritty focusing on alternatives. When you characterize your purchaser personas, you can make social promotions that talk straightforwardly to the intended interest group you have characterized. At that point, utilize social advertisement focusing to get your promotion before precisely the opportune individuals.

You can make separate advertisement content for every one of your characterized purchaser personas. This high-level degree of focusing on builds change rates and improves social promotion crusades.

3. Increment ROI with the purchaser persona spring

Created by educators and creators Aleksej Heinze, Gordon Fletcher, Tahir Rashid, Ana Cruz, the purchaser persona spring is a model for associating your business destinations to your purchaser persona. It's known as a spring since it includes three particular circles:

Content: What sorts of substance will address your purchaser persona?

Channels: What social channels does your purchaser persona utilize most?

Information: Good information permits you to screen your endeavors, report on your prosperity, and overhaul your methodology varying.

Each circle incorporates four focuses, at which you plan, act, notice, and reflect.

We'll dive into the subtleties of social occasion and arranging with this data in the following segment.

Step by step instructions to make a purchaser persona

Assemble your data as you work through these means. We've made a free purchaser persona format you can use to assemble it all when you will stage five.

1. Do exhaustive crowd research

Your purchaser personas should be founded on genuine information, not gut sense. Here's an essential outline of how to find out about your crowd. For a more top to bottom glance at these ideas, look at our total manual for crowd research.

Incorporate information on your current clients and social crowd

Consider subtleties like:

- Age
- Area
- Language
- spending force and examples
- Interests
- Difficulties
- Phase of life

For B2B, additionally, consider the size of the business and who settles on buying choices.

Accumulate this data from:

- Online media examination, particularly Facebook Audience Insights
- Your client information base
- Google Analytics
- Realize which social channels your crowd employments

You need to arrive at your clients utilizing the correct channels. Start by realizing where they as of now invest energy on the web. Some incredible apparatuses to help include:

Hootsuite Insights Powered by Brandwatch: Find top important destinations, hashtags, and creators

Keyhole.co: Find top alluding destinations for applicable hashtags

Google Analytics: See which interpersonal organizations show up in your reference traffic report

Look at the opposition

Follow the client research your rivals have just done, utilizing instruments like:

Buzzsumo: To look for top shared substance across interpersonal organizations, including commitment information.

Search streams: In your Hootsuite dashboard, set up streams to screen your rivals' posts and search for designs in hashtags, post sort, and substance procedure.

For more point by point systems, look at our full post on the best way to lead contender research utilizing social devices.

2. Distinguish client trouble spots

What issues or bothers are your potential clients attempting to address? What's keeping them away from progress? What obstructions do they face in arriving at their objectives?

One key approach to discover is to participate in some social tuning in and online media assessment investigation.

Setting up hunt streams to screen notices of your image, items, and contenders give you a continuous investigation of what individuals are stating about you on the web. You can realize why they love your items, or which parts of the client experience are simply not working.

It's likewise a smart thought to check in with your client support group to perceive what sorts of inquiries they get the most. See whether they can assist you with recognizing designs about which gatherings will in general face various types of difficulties. You could even request that they gather genuine client sites that you can use to help give your crowd personas profundity.

3. Recognize client objectives

This is the other side of trouble spots. Trouble spots are issues your potential clients are attempting to settle. Objectives or desires are positive things they need to accomplish.

Those objectives may be close to home or expert, contingent upon the sorts of items and administrations you sell. What spurs your clients? What's their end game?

These objectives may be straightforwardly identified with arrangements you can give, yet they don't need to be. This is more about becoming more acquainted with your clients than it is attempting to coordinate clients precisely to highlights or advantages of your item.

Your personas' objectives are significant regardless of whether they don't relate explicitly to your item's highlights. They can generally frame the premise of a mission, or they may basically illuminate the tone or approach you to take in your promoting.

Social listening can be a decent method to accumulate this data, as well. Also, similarly, as your client assistance group was a decent wellspring of understanding for problem areas, your outreach group can be a decent wellspring of knowledge on client objectives.

Your salesmen converse with genuine individuals who are contemplating utilizing your item. They have a profound comprehension of what your clients are attempting to accomplish by utilizing your items and administrations.

Request that they gather genuine statements that exemplify the client experience. You can likewise ask them for any strategies they use to beat purchaser complaints when selling your items or administrations, which drives us to...

4. See how you can help

Since you comprehend your clients' problem areas and objectives, it's an ideal opportunity to make a truly away from how your items and administration can help. As a component of this progression, you'll need to quit considering your image as far as highlights and burrow profound to investigate the advantages you offer to clients.

It tends to be difficult for advertisers to escape the element attitude—which is one explanation purchaser personas are so significant. They help you flip your reasoning and think about your items and administrations from a purchaser's perspective.

An element is a thing that your item is or does. An advantage is a manner by which your item or administration makes your client's life simpler or better.

Pose yourself three key inquiries for every one of the trouble spots and objectives you've gathered:

How might we help? Catch that in one clear sentence and add it to your persona layout.

What are your crowd's fundamental buying obstructions? What's more, how might you help beat them?

Where are your supporters in their purchasing venture? It is safe to say that they are investigating or prepared to purchase? Searching for surveys?

Once more, conversing with your associates who manage clients can be an incredible method to learn. It can likewise be a smart thought to counsel your clients and social fans straightforwardly through a study.

5. Make your purchaser personas

Presently, assemble the entirety of your exploration and begin searching for regular qualities. As you bunch those qualities together, you'll have the premise of your one of a kind client personas.

Suppose you recognize a center client gathering of fathers in their 30s who live in large urban communities, as to camp and possess cruisers. Incredible—presently it's an ideal opportunity to take this theoretical assortment of attributes and transform them into a persona that you can relate to and address.

Give your purchaser persona a name, a working title, a home, and other characterizing attributes. You need your persona to appear to be a genuine individual.

Focus on the measure of data you would hope to see on a dating site. Or on the other hand what you may gain from a short discussion on a plane or at a bus station. Remember to incorporate problem areas and objectives.

For instance, your gathering of cruisers claiming metropolitan father campers could be spoken to by the persona you name Moto Mike. In light of examination, you'll give Mike agent attributes that make him a genuine individual:

- He is 40 years of age
- He has two children, matured 4 and 1
- He lives in Boston
- He works at a tech organization
- He possesses a visiting cruiser
- He jumps at the chance to camp all through New England

He has restricted excursion time, Etc.

Keep in mind, a rundown of attributes doesn't approach a persona. A persona is a reasonable portrayal of an individual who speaks to one fragment of your client base.

Of course, not all individuals in this client bunch coordinate the qualities of your persona precisely. However, this persona speaks to this client gathering to you and permits you to consider them in a human manner as opposed to as an assortment of information focuses.

It's much simpler to address Mike than it is to address "men." Or even "35-year-old fathers who own cruisers."

As you tissue out your client personas, make certain to depict both who every persona is currently and who they need to be. This permits you to begin pondering how your items and administrations can assist them with getting a spot of desire.

3. Genuine purchaser persona models

1. Amsterdam Dance Event

The Amsterdam Dance Event (ADE) is a yearly electronic concert and meeting held in, you got it, Amsterdam.

A SurveyPlanet study appropriated through Facebook gave the structure squares to a purchaser persona with the accompanying attributes:

Matured 22 to 29

Dynamic via web-based media

Is an understudy or specialist

Has gone to ADE more than once

Goes to ADS to encounter electronic music with companions, meet similar individuals, and communicate

Has a medium degree of discretionary cashflow

Is value delicate for tickets an on-location spending

Nonetheless, with the goal for this to be a genuine purchaser persona, it would be considerably more explicit. Keep in mind, a purchaser persona ought to portray an individual, not simply a bunch of qualities. Thus, to take this to the following level, we should make a persona for ADE, following this ADE Facebook post.

Purchaser persona: Dancing Dave

27-year-old business understudy at the University of Amsterdam

A standard guest to nearby move clubs

Gone to ADE a year ago with two companions from school

Works low maintenance in the college library

Offers and likes pictures of Amsterdam's nightlife on Instagram Stories

Follows ADE on Facebook to be advised about prompt riser tickets

2. Fan Fit

Fan Fit is an application that outgrew a venture at the UK's University of Salford. It consolidates wellness following games news and long-range informal communication through close to home "associations." UK sports groups can Whitelabel the application to draw in their fans.

Two business educators worked with the application originators to character-ize their purchaser personas for a situation concentrate for the college where the application was made. What's more, these are extraordinary business educators. They're similar business educators who built up the purchaser persona spring referenced previously.

This is what they found:

Persona 1 (B2C): Jim Watson, an avid supporter

52-year-old van driver living in Salford with his significant other

Season ticket holder with Salford Red Devils

Devoted soccer fan

Utilizations TV, Twitter, Facebook, and YouTube

A previous competitor who has put on weight and pondered purchasing a wellness tracker however is uncertain what to purchase

Propelled to utilize a versatile application to improve wellbeing and personal satisfaction after a companion endured a minor coronary episode

In this Facebook video, two Fan Fit clients who are Salford Red Devils fans talk about the weight they've lost utilizing the group's variant of the application. They each state they've lost around three stone or around 40 pounds.

Persona 2 (B2B): Andrea Rogers, works in showcasing for a games group

Senior showcasing and correspondences rep for a significant soccer group

Deals with a little group of social advertisers

In her 30s and as of late wedded

Utilizations Facebook and Instagram to interface with her family, and Twitter and LinkedIn for proficient systems administration

Keen on applications, IoT, computer-generated reality, and eSports

Needs to associate the group with more youthful and more female fans

Is baffled that her group has no designs to fabricate its own application

3. HaparandaTornio Tourist Information Center

This travel industry office for the twin urban areas of Haparanda, Sweden, and Tornio, Finland, come up short on a reasonable computerized promoting system. A business organization understudy at the Lapland University of Applied Sciences worked with the travel industry focus to build up a group of people persona as a component of another advanced showcasing plan.

Purchaser persona: Maria Suomalainen

Brought into the world in Germany however, lives in Tornio

Matured 25 to 34 years with two youngsters

Goes with her family

Has a four-year certification

Utilizations the travel industry focus' site to search for occasions, eateries, spots to visit, and shops

Is disappointed by the place of interest's exhausting online media, absence of visual substance, and absence of communication with guests

Utilizations Facebook, Instagram, TripAdvisor, and Pinterest

Lean towards video, photograph, and text posts, alongside Instagram Stories

The Tourist Center is currently utilizing more visual substance, shares heaps of occasions, and has social offer catches for Twitter, Facebook, and Pinterest on its site.

One test with this purchaser persona: No individual is matured 25 to 34 years. While that age reach may portray the place of interest's intended interest group, the purchaser persona ought to have a particular age.

Consider your purchaser personas each time you settle on a choice about your web-based media substance and generally showcasing methodology. Do directly by these personas and you'll construct a bond with the genuine clients they speak to—boosting deals and brand reliability.

Share customer journey maps & conversation across the organization

Client venture planning is a method that is filling in fame, with client experience (CX) experts, yet additionally inside advertising, client assistance, client experience (UX), item the executives and IT. Client venture planning causes you to imagine your client's experience from the client's perspective, across all the distinctive touchpoints they have with your image as they look to accomplish a particular objective or objectives.

In this post, I'll clarify why client venture maps are arising as a successful correspondence, dynamic, and administration device, and survey five situations where they can fill in as an integral asset for changing your association.

There's both craftsmanship and science to making powerful travel maps. We should initially take a gander at a portion of the critical qualities of excursion guides, and why they are significant.

Excursion maps change complex information and bits of knowledge about your clients into a conservative, one-page visual portrayal. This minimized representation of key data makes venture maps simple to share and comprehend.

Client driven associations are utilizing venture guides to:

Set up a comprehensive comprehension of their client's present insight across touchpoints

Comprehend the "why" behind client conduct investigation and scorecards

Recognize the key "represent the deciding moment it" minutes in the general excursion

Recognize and organize occasions to improve the client experience

Envision a "future-state" client experience to spike development

Convey and adjust the association around a client-driven model

Fill in as a change the executives and administration apparatus

You can generally give more point by point reports and introductions to add profundity and subtlety to data introduced in an excursion map. You can even make numerous, related excursion guides to picture and convey all the significant subtleties of your clients' venture required for dynamic inside your association.

Use Customer Journey Mapping to Create a Storytelling and Decision Making Framework

The best excursion maps go past just catching and speaking to information in a visual arrangement to recount an anecdote about your client's experience from their viewpoint. They help to make sympathy for your clients AND backing development situated dynamic inside your association.

Day in the Life Journey Map Example

A 'Day in the Life' Journey Map recounts a story in a visual organization about your client's experience.

This implies that a choice cycle happens while interpreting the client experience information that has been gathered and picturing it in a guide. The level and sorts of subtleties you select to envision will rely upon your objectives for making the guide, who your partners are, and the particulars of your client's excursion.

Archive Customer Stages and Goals

Client venture maps utilize a phase model, where each stage speaks to a critical goal or objective in your client's general excursion. The excursion is made from the viewpoint of client needs, instead of from an interior, business measure system. The excursion stages and their connected objectives make the establishment of your excursion map and of how you think and discussion about your clients' excursion inside your association. This assists with moving speculation from a back to front to an outside-in mindset.

Excursion planning makes it simple to introduce basic client discoveries.

This move-in intuition from inside centered business cycles to remotely engaged client experience stages is a significant advance towards releasing the force of your association to drive development by making positive, noteworthy, client encounters.

While keeping an outside-in methodology, you can in any case imagine the connection between inner cycle steps and your client venture organizes by including both the 'front stage' and 'backstage' in a similar guide.

Catch Customer Feelings and Emotions

A vital aspect of understanding your client's experience is to see how their communications with your image cause them to feel. Is your image conveying encounters that produce positive encounters? Would your clients like to rehash the encounters they've had with your image?

The feelings clients have while connecting with your image are associated with their future practices—and those practices straightforwardly sway business development. Client assumptions for their collaborations with brands are getting progressively requesting and less lenient, as an ever-increasing number of organizations are conveying client encounters that genuinely improve their clients' lives. Excursion maps raise client feelings at key focuses in their excursion to the bleeding edge.

Chronicling client feelings is vital to building up an excursion map with an outside-in context.

Comprehend the Meaning Behind Customer Analytics

This subjective, humanistic point of view on your clients can assist you with understanding the why behind quantitative client investigation, scorecard information, and key business execution measurements. This can lead the best approach to more sure choices on where to organize speculation in the interest of involvement driven development.

Truth be told, you can incorporate key business measurements into your client venture map, so it fills in as a client experience dashboard. This reconciliation of subjective and quantitative information utilizing the excursion planning structure is an amazing method to move to a client arranged perspective on a social investigation, scorecard, and business execution information.

Your clients' communications with your image happen across various touch-points throughout their excursion. A touchpoint alludes to each purpose of association between your client and your image. On the off chance that you are a multi-channel retailer, for instance, every cooperation with your retail site, a business partner, a client assistance rep, and so forth, is viewed as a one of a kind touchpoint.

Most organizations are coordinated into self-governing working gatherings to deal with the intricate work of conveying the client experience at each touchpoint. Be that as it may, clients don't convey this inward model of your organization in their mind. They are centered around their own objectives and requirements as they collaborate with the numerous touchpoints in their excursion to meet those objectives and necessities. How your business is coordinated to convey those objectives and requirements is undetectable and immaterial to them.

In the past, it was normal for multi-channel retail shoppers to be stood up to with the way that the on the web and physical zones of their favored retailer were diverse business gatherings and were not composed for the client experience. Shoppers hesitantly acknowledged that reality, however, was left baffled.

Today, assumptions have changed because of inventive organizations that understood that they could improve their clients' lives by making their on the web and disconnected retail encounters totally consistent from their client's perspective, paying little heed to the inside association of the business bunches conveying these encounters. Significant retailers presently make it simple for clients to communicate with them across diverts in a consistent, brought together way—particularly at significant touchpoints in their excursion.

Excursion maps assist your association with seeing how and where clients cooperate with the distinctive touchpoints in their excursion. What's more, above all, they show how client's encounters at every one of those touchpoints sway their general involvement in your image. A helpless involvement with a key touchpoint can fundamentally affect your client's experience as they proceed in their excursion, fix positive encounters at prior touchpoints, or upset an excursion out and out.

This excursion map shows a client's touchpoint with a carrier.

Client venture planning causes you to recognize those significant touchpoints and organize speculation to make an encounter that will drive development, paying little heed to which business gatherings or gatherings are liable for conveying the encounters at those touchpoints.

Clients associate with your image since they are looking to address an issue or want. For instance, if you are a carrier, your client may have to go for business purposes and looks to have a movement experience that is proficient, adaptable, agreeable, and practical. They collaborate with your image with the assumption for addressing these necessities and wants and will keep on doing as such if you meet them in a manner that creates positive feelings. On the off chance that you don't, clients will try to address their issues somewhere else. It's as straightforward as that.

Effective organizations drive development by conveying encounters that address client issues in a manner that produce good feelings and leave clients feeling like they would need to rehash that experience. Thus, you need a compelling apparatus to help you settle on client experience that has driven choices to convey on this vision.

Client Journey Mapping Reinforces Customer-Driven Decision Making

As a business dynamic instrument, client venture maps bring client needs and assumptions to the front line of the discussion. They assist you with recognizing the main minutes in their excursion, see how your firm is conveying those key requirements and assumptions, and organize interest in client experience improvement undertakings to drive development.

Client driven development has gotten progressively significant as an ever-increasing number of organizations grasp this methodology and address the inside difficulties in their associations that hold up the traffic of conveying positive client encounters.

Client venture maps are a basic instrument to help your firm grasp this reality by moving the business dynamic system from customary business execution measurements to a client experience driven structure. By this, I mean utilizing your client venture as the edge or focal point through which you see your conventional business execution metric.

Excursion guides can be useful to individuals in various jobs and at various degrees of an association. How might travel maps help your association? Here are five circumstances where client venture planning can be utilized to change your association:

1. Spread a client-driven culture across your association

"CX achievement requires a solid craving for culture."

Top-down culture change is fundamental to make an effective client experience driven association. It's additionally testing. Here's top-notch of some regular ways CX pioneers, for example, Chief Customer Officers (CCOs), Chief Digital Officers (CDOs), and Chief Marketing Officers (CMOs) can utilize client venture planning to drive culture change:

initiative presentation2

Focus on it to include key influencers and partners across the association all through client venture planning endeavors.

Draw in pioneers all through the association, across storehouses, as key partners and colleagues to distinguish the main client journey(s) to demonstrate. This is a significant initial step for building joint efforts across storehouses.

Utilize an excursion guide to show the effect of client feelings on business execution. This should be set up with the goal for pioneers to be available to understand that the business measurements and scorecards commonly utilized in these situations just tell part of the presentation story.

Organize the key CX chances recognized in an advanced client venture map with authority across authoritative storehouses and utilize that as a beginning stage for making a vital guide for making changes.

Join forces with a particular specialty unit or other practical gatherings with your association to bore down on a particular stage or touchpoint in the general excursion. Thusly, you can more readily comprehend whether the item or administration they own is:

Affecting the client experience

Helpful as an apparatus for reconsidering the experience where it is missing the mark

Helpful for progressing administration of the progressions they make to the experience.

Work with chief administration to utilize your client venture planning structure as the beginning stages in authority gatherings, where business execution is being investigated, assessed, and followed upon. This is a basic advance to help your association move from a back to front culture to an outside-in culture.

2. Organize your specialty unit's ventures for the coming financial year to drive development

If you are a pioneer in a business bunch that claims the client experience for one channel and you need to organize your speculations throughout the following year, how might you guarantee that they're adjusted across the association?

Like you, the heads of different channels may accept that the connections across channels should be coordinated for the benefit of a consistent client experience. Notwithstanding sincere goals, without a proper instrument set up to encourage this kind of arranging every pioneer will make their own organized rundown lined up with their individual objectives and targets.

Your client venture guide can give a bound together focal point through which you and your associates can organize future speculations:

Make a client venture map that delineates the job at each touchpoint and divert play in the general client venture.

Your excursion map recognizes key minutes in the excursion where touch-points with your channel are disillusioning your clients.

Utilize your client venture map in your pre-key arranging discussions with your companions across the association. Specifically, utilize the guide in your discussions with channel pioneers where the client is out of sync with the involvement with their channel. They can undoubtedly comprehend the significance of changing the experience to be more consistent between the channels and the effect it will have on business development.

3. Revive the development of a current item

As an item proprietor, you may as of now be an enthusiastic devotee to a client-focused plan and your group may as of now utilize grounded strategies for consolidating iterative client criticism into the item technique and configu-ration measure. In any case, notwithstanding all the incredible work of your group, item development may not be the place where you need it to be. Client venture planning can assist you with reviving your item by empowering you to:

Collaborate with the cross-useful gatherings who uphold your item and make a client venture map. The guide will show the clients venture from item thought through buying it, utilizing it, and getting support.

Utilize the excursion guide to distinguish openings across all the distinctive useful zones and give setting to a portion of the known issues and help the group conceptualize the best way to tackle them.

Excursion Maps can assist you in restoring the development of a current item.

Excursion Maps can assist you in restoring the development of a current item.

4. Kick-off lead age for another item

A test numerous advertisers face when creating interest for another item is that you may not have a clue about a ton about your objective purchasers and how they assess and buy items like yours.

On the off chance that your showcasing bunch utilizes a lead age measure that was planned dependent on inner cycles and objectives, you will need to perceive what you could realize by utilizing the purchaser's excursion as the essential view. You can generally plan the inner cycle for the purchaser's travel and assess how well those cycles are serving the necessities of forthcoming clients. To adopt a purchaser centered strategy to lead age you can:

Commission an outsider to direct subjective exploration with existing and forthcoming clients to demonstrate the client venture from mindfulness, assessment, and buy through to starting onboarding, maintenance, and support.

Join forces with deals to approve and get purchase in.

Convey key bits of knowledge and things to do to your deals and client achievement groups, including where irregularities between practical regions are making rubbing for imminent purchasers.

5. Improve Voice of the Customer criticism

In the course of recent years, your organization may have put a great deal in get-together and refining client and business execution information. Provided that this is true, your administration group is likely inspired by and tunes in to Voice of the Customer (VOC) criticism.

As the VOC pioneer, you convey Net Promoter Scores (NPS), consumer loyalty input on explicit touchpoints, and client verbatims winnowed from the reviews. Scorecards are conveyed by channel, specialty units, and business measures. At whatever point conceivable, your group coordinates key scorecard measurements with client experiences separated from other client research contemplates, both subjective and quantitative, to give an extra setting.

Notwithstanding this client understanding, your association might be attempting to convey a client experience that is driving the focus on the degree of development. Assuming this is the case, you can:

Recognize and work together with a CX tactician or outside accomplice to convey a client venture map that models the client venture across all the significant phases of their relationship with your organization.

Utilize the subsequent client venture guide to adjust the Voice of the Customer scorecards you convey to the chief and specialty unit initiative group to report information by client stage, at whatever point conceivable.

Empower the authority groups to consider VOC information through the perspective of the client and to consider how those scores identify with the client experience story—and central issues of pleasure and contact—in their excursion.

End

Driving associations are currently hoping to separate themselves from their opposition by conveying an excellent client experience. Client venture maps are worked from the client's viewpoint, use objective-based stages as the system, envision your client's communications with your image across various touchpoints, and distinguish the feelings they are encountering all through the excursion. Excursion maps are a device for chronicling the client experience from an outside-in context and introducing them in a genuine, drawing in, and significant way—which makes them an ideal device for changing your organization into a really client-driven association.

12

How to reward customer for appreciation

Is it accurate to say that you are appreciative of your clients? Obviously, you are. The genuine inquiry is – do you show it? Client thankfulness assumes a significant job in holding clients. Examination shows 68% of clients change brands because of "saw detachment." at the end of the day, clients felt like the business couldn't have cared less on the off chance that they shopped with them or not.

What's the arrangement? Organizations should show a little love. To help time-lashed entrepreneurs show client gratefulness, here's a top-notch of approaches to state thank you to the clients who keep your business running.

1. Offer an unwaveringness program with layered prizes

There's no simpler method to show your gratefulness to clients than to compensate them through a dependability program – and an extraordinary ole devotion program – one that offers numerous motivations and prizes. As clients purchase from you, they acquire focuses that can be utilized towards a few items or administrations that they truly need.

2. Make a gift in their honor

Make a gift to a neighborhood noble cause to pay tribute to your most faithful clients. Send them a book or an email to tell them the uplifting news. Show nearby clients that as they uphold you, they additionally uphold the local area.

3. Give an overhaul

Treat clients to a redesign. If you offer an administration, knock them up an indent. In case you're offering an exceptional markdown on a thing, offer a more profound rebate to your faithful clients.

4. Giveaway candy favors

Head to the store, snatch some treats and extravagant plastic packs and make your own "Thank You" favors. Or on the other hand, fill the baggies with tests from your own business. Give the treats out at the counter, or send them via the post office for a remarkable turn.

5. Host an outing or BBQ

Consider facilitating a client excursion or BBQ. You can have it at a local area park, or right outside of your business. Collaborate with neighboring organizations to make it a square wide occasion.

6. Commend an achievement

As you construct a relationship with clients, make certain to gather data about them. That way, you can send extraordinary proposals on their birthday or the commemoration that they pursued your private company unwaveringness program.

7. Part with a little loot

Request a little loot for your clients and part with it in-store with each buy. It doesn't need to be as conventional as a free pen. Go for something like a lip analgesic or a water bottle.

8. Send a transcribed note

In an advanced world, transcribed notes show you give it a second thought. They're an incredible alternative for deals and administration based organizations. Send a thank you after a deal, or in the wake of finishing an administration for a first-time client.

9. Treat a client

Each once in for some time, give a reliable client an unforeseen rebate at the checkout. Possibly you comp a client's espresso or give a client an additional 10% off because.

10. Highlight clients on social

Give clients a yell out via web-based media. Pick a "Devotee of the Week" and highlight a brisk Q and A with them, or offer their motivating story like the Red Cross does with this post from a bosom malignant growth survivor:

11. Free vehicle wash

Set up a free vehicle wash on a Saturday evening for your clients. Request that staff volunteer for the occasion, or collaborate with a neighborhood sports group. Make a gift to the group in return for their assistance with the occasion.

12. Highlight clients available

Pick a client at arbitrary every week, snap their image, and make them the Customer of the Week. Balance their image on a unique notice board behind the register.

13. Meet with clients off-site

Express profound gratitude by taking a client out to espresso or lunch. It's not something you'll accomplish for each client, but rather it's a pleasant method to show thankfulness for those exceptional rare sorts of people who belittle your business habitually.

14. Host drawings with the expectation of complimentary stuff

Host client gratefulness giveaways. It tends to be as straightforward as requesting that clients drop their business card in a bowl for an opportunity to win a free lunch, or request some cool lottery-like cards that give irregular clients a possibility at a free thing or a major rebate.

15. Send an occasion blessing

Consider giving clients an unconditional present around the special seasons, or when your store arrives at a specific achievement, similar to a 10-year commemoration.

16. Night-time deal

Treat a little gathering of clients to a twilight deal. Let your new clients or your VIPs come in for an hour after you near shop an uncommon deal. It's an incredible opportunity to become more acquainted with your clients as well. Get familiar with their names and start discussions with them.

17. Celebrity treatment

Think about giving the first-class reception – in a real sense. Have additional staff close by to take into account all clients' impulses for a day. For retailers, have representatives invite clients, offer them a drink, and convey their sacks to their vehicle. Make an occasion out of it, and deal with every client like a

VIP.

18. Make a thank you video

Get the entire organization included and make a thank you video. Here's an extraordinary model from the email advertising organization, Constant Contact. At the point when you're done, share it via web-based media and play it on a TV in your store.

13

Use an integrated marketing campaign

Coordinated advertising is the way toward masterminding your distinctive showcasing directs to work pair to advance your items or administrations, normally through an essential mission. Incorporated showcasing additionally attempts to adjust the essential brand message that is being conveyed through your promoting channels and resources.

Envision finding another brand on Instagram and visiting the organization's site to buy one of their items. On the off chance that their site advanced an alternate message or mission than the one you found on their Instagram account, you'd struggle to understand the substance of the brand, correct?

Incorporated promoting exists to kill these aberrations and contrasts paying little mind to how or when a client cooperates with your image. It's like multi-channel promoting, aside from coordinated showcasing is the thing that adjusts the message you're sharing on those channels.

Talking about channels, incorporated promoting doesn't matter to simply your inbound or computerized showcasing channels; customary media channels are additionally included. Large numbers of the coordinated showcasing models we'll audit beneath consolidate conventional advertising channels, for example, print, radio, and TV advertisements.

Presently, we should discuss incorporated advertising efforts.

Why are coordinated showcasing efforts successful?

While incorporated advertising efforts can contrast in their objectives (for example changing over perspectives, building brand mindfulness, and so on), they should all share one segment for all intents and purpose: to adjust your showcasing channels to introduce an assembled advertising "front".

If your promoting channels are players, consider your incorporated advertising effort the mentor accountable for running plays and aiding your channels fill in as a brought together framework — not different ones.

It's additionally more successful to run incorporated promoting efforts when contrasted with crusades on individual channels. Incorporated advertising efforts are effective for a couple of reasons:

They contact a more extensive crowd than a solitary promoting channel.

They have a more prominent possibility of being seen on numerous channels, hence keeping your image top-of-brain and pushing guests closer to transformation.

They fabricate trust with guests as they see a reliable message on various channels.

They set aside your cash since resources can be divided among and repurposed for various showcasing channels and, contingent upon your mission, clients can help you market your item or administration for you.

Build up your general mission objective

Pick your showcasing channels and set objectives for every one

Characterize your purchaser personas by channel

Distinguish your channel supervisors

Make versatile showcasing resources and informing

Set up your arrangement for gathering leads

Dispatch, measure and emphasize your mission

Anyway, how might you assemble your own coordinated promoting effort? Follow these means to begin.

1. Build up your general mission objective.

Before you consider what channels will be important for your incorporated advertising effort, you should think about the objective of the whole mission.

Perhaps you've dispatched another item, administration, or activity and need to get it before clients — like Southwest's Transparency. Possibly you've totally rebranded and need to communicate your new message — like Old Spice's Smell Like a Man, Man. Maybe you've basically picked another situating slogan and need your crowd to begin connecting your image with it — like Snickers' You're Not You When You're Hungry.

(Try not to stress, we'll dive further into these models later.)

Whatever your mission objective might be, consistently make sure to make it SMART. This will help you stay centered, track your mission achievement, and figure out how to improve the following time around.

These objectives ought to likewise identify with at any rate one of the accompanying key exhibition markers (KPIs) and their resulting measurements, which you can follow when you dispatch your mission.

Additionally, while expanded commitment and new leads are continually energizing, a multi-channel mission ought to likewise think about the master plan: how your mission impacts deal openings and business income. Pause for a minute to outline how you need your mission to affect your primary concern, as well.

2. Pick your showcasing channels and set objectives for everyone.

Since you realize you are all-encompassing incorporated promoting effort objective, you likely have a superior thought of what channels (if not every one of them) can help you arrive at that objective.

For instance, if you will likely reveal another logo and marking suite, you don't really have to use radio promotions. Then again, in case you're stretching out your crowd to focus on another geographic area or city, radio advertisements, announcement promotions, TV promotions, and other nearby diverts may prove to be useful.

While picking your channel(s), everything reduces to what exactly you're attempting to accomplish through your coordinated promoting effort. There are 10 significant advertising "channels" that you can use to convey your mission content.

Publicizing (both print and PPC)

Direct showcasing

Email showcasing

PR

Individual selling

Deals advancements

Computerized promoting (for example site, content promoting, and SEO)

Web-based media

Occasions and sponsorships

Bundling

Your coordinated advertising effort ought to remember an assortment of promoting channels for the request to contact the amplest crowd and commute home your mission message. On the off chance that you see at least one channel level, don't stop for a second to add, eliminate, or test new ones.

3. Characterize your purchaser personas by channel.

Each promoting channel focuses on its own particular purchaser persona. Hence, rather than characterizing an expansive persona for your mission, you should characterize your crowd by channel.

There will unavoidably be some cover, however, it's shrewd to see precisely who you're conversing with on every medium and how you can tailor those particular resources to be the best.

Note: for certain missions, you might be focusing on a particular crowd. For this situation, stages 2 and 3 would be flipped — you'd characterize your purchaser persona(s) first and afterward choose which channels can help you contact that crowd.

4. Recognize your channel chiefs.

Contingent upon the size of your showcasing group, you may have various individuals (or whole groups) accountable for various channels. When running a multi-channel showcasing effort, you should figure out who explicitly will be accountable for guaranteeing their channel(s) is lined up with the mission.

This is significant for two reasons: 1) that administrator is the master on their channel (for example crowd, posting rhythm, advancement strategies, revealing techniques, and so forth) and will realize how to tailor the mission substance to be the best; and 2) placing one individual accountable for all channels might be overpowering and will make the substance and mission endure.

Maybe you have a more modest showcasing group where one individual handles different channels. Notwithstanding your group size, do your absolute best to share channel the board duties across a couple of individuals — in a perfect world with one individual taking care of a couple of channels.

5. Make versatile promoting resources and informing.

Now, you have your mission objective, target audience(s), and promoting channels. It's currently an ideal opportunity to make your incorporated advertising effort content. This stage is the place where copywriting, visual communication, and other innovative cycles become possibly the most important factor.

Before I plunge into how we should discuss a significant part of coordinated showcasing content: versatility. To keep your mission reliable (and facilitate your outstanding burden), you ought to have the option to repurpose any substance to be utilized on various channels.

For instance, suppose your incorporated advertising effort is centered around the dispatch of another 3-minute brand video. You could repurpose this video into:

30-second and one-minute "trailer" recordings

Still pictures

Statements

GIFs

Hashtags

Blog entries

Audio clips

As you create and repurpose these imaginative resources, keep them lined up with your image rules and predictable with one another. Indeed, it very well might be useful to make your own arrangement of brand rules for your incorporated advertising effort to impart to your group and any channel supervisors.

This documentation could incorporate a couple of things:

Visual rules (logo, shading palette, typography, and so on)

Any created and repurposed resources in different document designs

Voice and tone rules (slogans, favored language, words to stay away from, and so on)

Informing rules (trouble spots, objectives, sorts of substance, assets, and so forth)

Purchaser persona data and rules

Incorporated promoting is about a steady brand insight. Be certain your mission resources mirror that, paying little heed to what channel your crowd visits or sees.

6. Set up your arrangement for gathering leads.

Regardless of whether you plan your mission to gather drives, you ought to consistently be set up to get them. You would prefer not to leave this as an untimely idea once you dispatch your mission. Regardless of whether you're basically crusading to bring issues to light of your image, consider how your guests may change over to leads — and, in the long run, clients.

To begin with, think about how a guest would change over to a lead. Would they buy into your bulletin? Info their data to download a substance offer? Make a record on your site? Guarantee these transformation parts of your mission are additionally on-brand with the remainder of your visual and informing resources.

Next, consider how your leads will be supported once they convert. Would they fold into a computerized email work process? Would you give them to Sales? Any way you approach this progression, ensure your leads aren't failed to remember once they readily give over their data.

As usual, speak with Sales to affirm that they're mindful of your mission and energetic about your arrangement for new leads and clients.

7. Dispatch, measure, and repeat your mission.

Prepared to dispatch your coordinated advertising effort? It very well may be an ideal opportunity to give your mission something to do ... however it's no chance to rest right now.

Recall those KPIs and measurements from stage one? Whichever KPIs identify with your overall mission objective (for example boosting brand mindfulness, rebranding, new item, and so forth), begin following those resulting measurements every week, month, and a quarter (contingent upon how long your mission is hurrying) to perceive how fruitful it is at arriving at your objective.

As usual, take what you gain from each coordinated showcasing crusade and apply it to future missions. With the correct methodologies, administrators, and apparatuses set up, you can make a ceaseless pattern of coordinated advertising efforts — and wins.

Coordinated Marketing Strategies and Best Practices

As you build your incorporated promoting effort, there are a couple of key systems and best practices to remember. We've itemized them here, and they apply paying little mind to what media, channels, or objectives you've picked.

Adjust Behind the Scenes

With the goal for you to effectively actualize a coordinated promoting approach, it's basic that you pick advertising channel administrators as well as that all your showcasing chiefs likewise convey regularly about tasks and missions.

While only one out of every odd coordinated showcasing effort or advancement should be on the entirety of your channels, they ought to at any rate supplement each other to dodge a divided brand insight for clients.

Consider the Channel Transition

Incorporated missions get traffic from various sources — and pass along those sources like a round of Hot Potato. Think about how a guest may see/experience each advertising channel 1) if it was their first visit and 2) on the off chance that they changed from another channel. Consider how each channel can help other people convert.

For instance, say a client saw your new board on their approach to work and, when they showed up, visited the site that was on the announcement. Envision if, on your site, the client couldn't undoubtedly discover whatever your board was advertising. How confounding could that be? That client would almost certainly drop off right away.

Try not to Neglect the Small Overlaps

When planning to dispatch your incorporated showcasing effort, it's enticing to independently consider each channel and its particular media resources. In any case, this point of view characteristically conflicts with the ethos of coordinated advertising. Coordinated showcasing exists to kill the storehouses of conventional advertising and unite a strong mission experience.

Hence, don't disregard the spots wherein your mission covers. Here are a couple of models:

Your email signature, where you can plug your online media handles, site URL, or video joins

Your online media profiles and posts, where you can incorporate connections to your site, blog entries, content offers, or other computerized content

Your blog and site, where you can consolidate social sharing catches

Your independent greeting pages, where you can streamline for important catchphrases and SEO

Your PPC duplicate, where you can guinea pig lines to perceive what your crowd reacts to

While these covers may not straightforwardly uphold your mission objectives, they help your crowd progress flawlessly between channels, appreciate that predictable, firm brand insight, and at last discover their way to a page that changes over them.

14

Be a leader in need-driven marketing

There's nobody "right" approach to lead a business. The present chiefs have a great deal of insight to grant about dealing with the cutting edge labor force because of every one methodologies initiative in their own remarkable manner. Consistently, Business News Daily will share an initiative exercise from a fruitful entrepreneur or leader.

The pioneer: Leslie Stretch, president, and CEO of CallidusCloud

Time in current position: 9 years

Leslie's way of thinking: "Supplant sense of self-driven initiative with client-driven administration."

The overall influence among clients and vender has moved. The present clients request that we don't just make surmises about their requirements and wants – we should work as really client-driven associations. Furthermore, if your organization will do that, you should supplant inner self-driven administration with client-driven authority.

I don't get that's meaning? Business pioneers should quit making moves dependent on what they feel – their hunches, instinct, and most realistic estimations about the correct moves for their associations – and rather act cooperatively with the individuals they offer to – and the information produced during the business cycle – to ensure the best results for those clients.

Organizations have studied their clients for an extremely prolonged stretch of time, yet a lot of that input frequently went unused or was overlooked. That can't proceed – purchasers presently expect that any criticism they offer will be thought of and followed up on to better their encounters as clients. The present examination innovation permits client input to be gathered, recorded, and broke down consequently; chiefs can comprehend customers' opinions and follow up on genuine information, as opposed to following up on hunches.

They can likewise demand that the voice of the client (VOC) is better coordinated into each part of the association. For example, the client's contribution to the nature of a business association ought to affect pay, since a decent deals experience makes way for more noteworthy reliability and a more extended and more productive client lifecycle.

While the innovation to add an information-driven measurement to client-driven administration is proceeding to acquire power, it's just a single piece of the condition. The other part is the ability to listen straightforwardly to clients. You should do this in two ways. To begin with, you need to effectively encourage conversation with clients you recognize deliberately, in light of segment, vertical market, and business case information. We do that through various client occasions the world over and through our client warning sheets (CABs). Furthermore, you need to keep channels open to get with a client who may not be important for that first gathering and who may communicate their suppositions employing your local area, on another online media channel, during discussions with one another in open discussions, or in discussions with your help group.

Obviously, such an excess of listening is an unsettled issue on the off chance that you don't have a cycle to disguise what clients are stating and use it to impact the heading of your organization, its items, and its arrangements. Each piece of the organization – deals, advertising, client assistance, and even item advancement and account – ought to have a bunch of obvious techniques for gathering and following up on the longings clients express. This activity should come starting from the top; the information you gather and the client channels you open should arrive at the highest point of the association. On the off chance that that client center is broken around the path to the CEO, you power workers to accommodate the inner self-driven impression of heads with this present reality worries of the client, an almost outlandish errand.

This client-driven methodology, not the slightest bit implies that you surrender control of your guide to clients. Or maybe, it moves the CEO to offset the business' advantages with an educated arrangement regarding the clients' advantages to be better lined up with their requirements, wants, and wishes. By doing that, your business can situate itself as a superior accomplice for your clients' prosperity, cultivate dedication, win a piece of the pie and drive more income over the long haul.

15

Prioritize segmentation, targeting, positioning, and differentiation

Today, Segmentation, Targeting, and Positioning (STP) is a recognizable vital methodology in Modern Marketing. It is quite possibly the most usually applied showcasing models practically speaking. In our survey getting some information about the most famous advertising model, it is the second generally mainstream, just beaten by the respected SWOT/TOWs network. This prevalence is generally later since already, showcasing approaches were based more around items as opposed to clients. During the 1950s, for instance, the primary promoting methodology was 'item separation'.

The STP model is valuable when making advertising correspondence plans since it causes advertisers to organize suggestions and afterward create and convey customized and significant messages to draw in with various audiences. stp-model this is a crowd of people instead of an item engaged way to deal with interchanges which convey more pertinent messages to financially engaging crowds. The outline underneath shows how plans can have the stream from

Applying Segmentation, Targeting, and Positioning to advanced interchanges

STP applies to advanced advertising too at a more strategic interchanges level. For instance, applying advertising personas can help grow more pertinent advanced interchanges as appeared by these option strategic email client division draws near. This visual from Dave Chaffey of Smart Insights in his book Digital Marketing: Strategy. Execution and practice show how Segmentation, Targeting, and Positioning apply to computerized advertising system.

It reminds us how advanced channels offer new choices for focusing on crowds that weren't accessible beforehand, yet we need to hold an adequate spending plan for. For instance:

Search expectation as searchers type watchwords when contrasting items they are keen on purchasing

Interest-based focusing on Facebook, for example Prospecting for those keen on Gardening, Gym participation or Golf

Focusing through email personalization and on-location personalization dependent on profile, conduct (for example content burned-through)

This post by Dave Chaffey has instances of 6 layered focusing on choices for email advertising which show how the hypothesis of vital division and focusing on can convert into strategic division and focusing on.

There are additionally new occasions to make a brand all the more convincing through contribution new kinds of significant worth to customers dependent on an on the web or advanced incentive or what Jay Baer has called Youtility. This can be employing substance or intelligent devices on sites or versatile applications.

How to utilize STP?

Through division, you can recognize specialties with explicit necessities, develop markets to discover new clients, convey more engaged and compelling promoting messages.

The necessities of each portion are the equivalent, so promoting messages ought to be intended for each fragment to stress applicable advantages and highlights required instead of one size fits for all client types. This methodology is more proficient, conveying the correct blend to a similar gathering of individuals, as opposed to a scattergun approach.

You can section your current business sectors dependent on almost any factor, as long as it's compelling as the models beneath show:

Notable approaches to portion your crowd include:

1. Socioeconomics

Breakdown by any mix: age, sex, pay, instruction, identity, conjugal status, training, family unit (or business), size, length of home, kind of home or even calling/Occupation.

A model is Firefox who sells 'coolest things', focused on a more youthful male crowd. However, Moshi Monsters, be that as it may, is focused on guardians with fun, protected, and instructive space for a more youthful crowd.

2. Psychographics

This alludes to 'character and feelings depends on conduct, connected to buy decisions, including perspectives, way of life, pastimes, hazard avoidance, character, and initiative qualities. magazines read and TV. While socioeconomics clarifies 'who' your purchaser is, psychographics educate you 'why' your client purchases.

There are a couple of various ways you can assemble information to help structure psychographic profiles for your average clients.

Meetings: Talk to a couple of individuals that are comprehensively illustrative of your intended interest group. Inside and out meetings let you accumulate valuable subjective information to truly comprehend what really matters to your clients. The issue is they can be costly and hard to direct, and the little example size implies they may not generally be illustrative individuals you are attempting to target.

Reviews: Surveys let you contact a bigger number of individuals than interviews, yet it very well may be more diligently to find clever solutions.

Client information: You may have information on what your clients will in general buy from you, for example, information coming from dedication cards if an FMCG brand or from online buy history on the off chance that you are an internet business. You can utilize this information to create experiences into what sort of items your clients are keen on and what is probably going to make them buy. For instance, does limiting boundlessly expand their affinity to buy? In which case they may be very unconstrained.

A model is Virgin Holidays who section occasions into 6 gatherings.

3. Way of life

This alludes to Hobbies, sporting pursuits, diversion, excursions, and other non-work time pursuits.

Organizations, for example, here and there line magazine will focus on those with explicit interests for example FourFourTwo for football fans.

A few interests are huge and grounded, and accordingly generally simple to target, for example, the football fan model. Be that as it may, a few organizations have discovered incredible achievement focusing on little specialties successfully. An incredible model is a blast in 'preparing' related organizations, which has gone from somewhat known about periphery action to a billion-dollar industry lately. Obviously now 3.7 million American's consider themselves preppers or survivalists. An extraordinary method to begin researching and focusing on this sort of specialty is Reddit, where individuals make subReddits to share data about a given interest or diversion.

4. Conviction and Values

Alludes to Religious, political, nationalistic, and social convictions and qualities.

The Islamic Bank of Britain offers Sharia-agreeable financial which meets explicit strict necessities.

A bizarre however intriguing illustration of strict socioeconomics impacting showcasing that you probably won't have speculated is that Mormons are truly into 'staggered advertising'. They're definitely bound to be occupied with the training than some other US gathering. Going the additional mile with segment examination can prompt finding new advertising openings and breaking new ground. For instance, did you know 55-64-year-olds are the most probable age gathering to purchase another vehicle? Be that as it may, you don't in general see them in the vehicle promotions. A chance holding back to be seized!

5. Life Stages

Life Stages is the Chronological benchmarking of individuals' lives at various stages.

A model is Saga occasions which are just accessible for individuals matured 50+. They guarantee a huge enough section to zero in on this life stage.

6. Topography

Drill somewhere around Country, district, region, metropolitan or provincial area, populace thickness, or even atmosphere.

A model is Neiman Marcus, the upmarket retail chain in the USA currently conveys to the UK.

7. Conduct

Alludes to the idea of the buy, brand unwaveringness, utilization level, benefits looked for, dispersion channels utilized, response to advertising factors.

In a B2B climate, the advantages looked for are regularly about 'how before long would it be able to be conveyed?' which incorporates the 'latest possible time' fragment – the arranging ahead of the time portion.

A model is Parcelmonkey.co.uk who offer same day, following day, and global bundle conveyances.

8. Advantage

The advantage is the utilization and fulfillment acquired by the buyer.

Smythson Stationery offers comparable items to other writing material organizations, yet their customers need the advantage of their unmistakable bundling: tissue-fixed Nile Blue boxes and attached with naval force lace!

Market focusing on

The rundown underneath alludes to what in particular's expected to assess the potential and business appeal of each section.

Models Size: The market should be sufficiently enormous to legitimize dividing. If the market is little, it might make it more modest.

Distinction: Measurable contrasts should exist between fragments.

Cash: Anticipated benefits should surpass the expenses of extra advertising plans and different changes.

Open: Each fragment should be available to your group and the portion should have the option to get your advertising messages

Zero in on various advantages: Different fragments should require various advantages.

Item situating

Situating maps are the last component of the STP cycle. For everything to fall into place, you need two factors to outline the market review.

In the model here, I've taken a few vehicles accessible in the UK. This is anything but an itemized item position map, a greater amount of an outline. If there were no vehicles in a single portion it could demonstrate a market opportunity.

Developing the amazingly essential model above, you can unload the market by planning your rivals onto a lattice dependent on key factors that decide buy.

This diagram isn't intended to be any sort of exact portrayal of the vehicle market, but instead delineate how you could utilize an item situating guide to dissect your own organization's current situation on the lookout, and distinguish openings. For instance, as you can find in the hole underneath, we've distinguished in a potential chance on the lookout for low-evaluated family vehicles.

We're not saying this hole really exists, I'm certain you could consider vehicles that fit this classification, as the vehicle market is a very evolved and serious market. Notwithstanding, it shows how you can utilize the device to recognize holes in your own market.

Any time you suspect there are critical, quantifiable contrasts in your market, you ought to think about STP. Particularly on the off chance that you need to make a scope of various directives for various gatherings.

16

Now go reverse starting from your customer need

Conveying a phenomenal client experience is the very pinnacle of significance in the current business climate. Indeed, as indicated by ongoing examination did by Podium, 68 percent of buyers are happy to pay 15 percent more for precisely the same item on the off chance that they can ensure a superior involvement with the cycle.

It is not, at this point enough to just contend dependent on items and cost. All things being equal, client experience is one of the greatest serious differentiators, which is the reason organizations organize building up the client assistance abilities of their groups through methods like client assistance instructing and preparing.

Probably the most ideal approach to guarantee the client experience is positive is to embrace a procedure dependent on tackling issues for clients and putting client needs upfront. Here, we investigate the 'working in reverse's technique for client encounters and clarify how it tends to be helpful for your business and its standing.

Characterizing 'Working Backwards'

In basic terms, the 'working in reverse' technique can be portrayed as beginning with a client's need, need, or issue and answering an item, administration, or experience. The option includes beginning with an item, highlight, or arrangement and attempting to discover a crowd of people for it.

The most popular advocate of the 'working in reverse' strategy was Steve Jobs. In 1997, at the Apple World Wide Developers Conference, Jobs utilized the fundamental hypothesis to react to an affront from a group of people part, who blamed him for not completely understanding the innovation he was examining.

"Something I've generally found is that you must be beginning with the client experience and work in reverse to the innovation," Jobs stated, laying out his vision. "You can't begin with the innovation and attempt to sort out where you will attempt to sell it. A few missteps will be made en route... and we'll fix them."

This statement summarizes the essential way of thinking behind the technique. By beginning with the issue or need, you can work in reverse to discover an answer and afterward offer it to clients. This shouldn't be restricted exclusively to the items or administrations you sell. Consider client needs, needs, and assumptions at each phase of their purchasing venture. What do they need from your site? What do they need from an in-store visit? At that point think about the arrangement.

Embracing the Strategy

Perhaps the main part of really actualizing a 'working in reverse's strategy is distinguishing precisely what is needed from the client experience. You ought not to depend on mystery for this. All things considered, you ought to address clients consistently, discover what they need, find out about their difficulties, and distinguish explicit necessities.

As Dave Bailey brings up in an article for Inc.com, it is additionally fundamental that, when speaking with clients, you lead with the need. This means when you portray an item or an administration, or a specific component, you start by clarifying what needs its locations and afterward clarify how it does this. It is critical to require some investment to do this, regardless of whether this implies contextualizing the need itself first, which is regularly the situation.

Furthermore, your business ought to persistently search out criticism from clients and measure execution against client assumptions. This data ought to likewise be utilized to advise client support instructing endeavors.

"Measure the client experience by gathering quantitative and subjective data straightforwardly from clients," says Seleste Lunsford, the Managing Director at CSO Insights, in a blog entry on conveying an elite client experience. "Don't simply make suppositions on whether you are satisfying what you guarantee. Inquire."

Understanding the Benefits

A critical advantage of this strategy is that it permits client care abilities, promoting messages and deals data to be based around the necessities being tended to, as opposed to the items or highlights being sold, making it all the more quickly applicable to clients. As a result, clients feel they are being served, instead of offered to.

This, thus, assists with making a feeling that your business really needs to help clients. Besides, it makes it simpler to impart the real genuine estimation of the item or administration being talked about, as opposed to attempting to underline viewpoints that may require specialized information.

At long last, the 'working in reverse's strategy additionally shows a specific degree of compassion and proposes your business has really pondered how clients or customers feel and what their interests are.

"It can eventually build reliability and maintenance," says Nikki Gilliland, composing for Econsultancy. "By indicating more noteworthy consciousness of the client's necessities and trouble spots, brands can make an enthusiastic association with a crowd of people instead of a simply value-based or useful one."

End

The 'working in reverse' way to deal with client experience, pushed by any semblance of Steve Jobs, includes utilizing client needs and needs as the beginning stage and afterward working in reverse to convey answers for issues. Accordingly, it can make your items, administrations, and different deals work more applicable to clients.

From that point, clients are bound to build up a proclivity for your business, feel as though you have their inclinations on a fundamental level and advantage from a good generally speaking client experience.